THE
EASY WAY TO
BIRD
RECOGNITION

THE
EASY WAY TO
BIRD
RECOGNITION

JOHN KILBRACKEN

Kingfisher Books

Kingfisher Books, Grisewood & Dempsey Ltd,
Elsley House, 24–30 Great Titchfield Street,
London W1P 7AD

This edition first published in 1989 by Kingfisher Books
10 9 8 7 6
Originally published in hardcover in 1982

BRITISH LIBRARY CATALOGUING IN PUBLICATION DATA
Kilbracken, John Godley, *Baron, 1920–*
The easy way to bird recognition
1. Great Britain. Birds
I. Title
598.2941
ISBN 0 86272 397 3

Design by Adrian Hodgkins
Cover illustration by Terence Lambert
Illustrations by Martin Camm, Bernard Robinson and
David Wright
Phototypeset by Southern Positives and Negatives (SPAN),
Lingfield, Surrey
Printed in Italy by Vallardi Industrie Grafiche, Milan

How to Use this Book

This book has only one purpose – to make it easier than ever before to identify, as quickly as possible, all the birds you are most likely to see in the British Isles.

It's no good pretending that bird recognition can be made easy in every case. There are too many species, often with only minor differences, for that. No book can enable you to distinguish every small brown bird you glimpse vanishing into the undergrowth.

But the use of a simple systematic key, and the restriction of the main part of the book to the 184 species that occur most often in the British Isles, will make it possible for you to put a name to almost any bird you have been able to watch carefully. A supplementary list at the back of the book covers another 38 rarer species.

Here's how the book works. It consists of 290 Questions and Answers. The former are numbered in blue, the latter in yellow. You always start off at 1. You then turn in sequence to each successive Question indicated. These are so chosen that you should have the least possible difficulty in deciding on each reply. A few lines of text are always included to help you.

After perhaps as few as three Questions, and never more than a dozen, you will arrive at an Answer. This lists the species – sometimes only one species, never more than four – amongst which your bird is almost sure to be. Illustrations in the margin, and another passage of text, make it easy for you to decide between them.

If you do not find your bird in the main part of the book, turn to the supplementary list at the end, where the less common species are set out. If it is not amongst them, you have either made a mistake and should start again at the beginning, or you have spotted a real rarity and should consult a more comprehensive bird book. The only other possibility – especially in the summer – is that the bird was a juvenile. Juveniles usually differ from adults, but present too many difficulties for inclusion.

Now let's take an example of how to use the book. Imagine that you have seen in woodland a small bird with a bright yellow breast and a blue head – that's all you had time to notice. Starting at 1, you have no trouble in deciding it was a *land bird*, which leads you on to 2.

Here you again read the instructions, and decide at once that it was *chaffinch-size or smaller* – not more than 15cm from beak to tail. This leads you to 3. You choose *yellow* as the predominant colour and therefore turn to 59. The bird may have been small, but it was more than a mere 9cm in length, so you go on to 61.

The text leads you to realize that it was indeed *a member of the tit family* and you turn to 62, which you see at once is your Answer. Two choices are offered, the great tit and the blue tit. The illustrations in the margin, and the text accompanying them, leave you in no doubt that it must have been a blue tit.

In many cases there are 'overlaps'. By this I mean that the same solution can be reached by several different routes, if you make a small mistake or if any doubt exists about the correctness of a reply. For instance, in the example just given, you might have thought that blue was the predominant colour in preference to yellow. This would have led you at once to 62 with the same outcome.

And if, for instance, the bird had been very close in size to a chaffinch, you would have reached the correct solution whichever reply you chose to 2.

Water birds that are sometimes seen far from water are included among the land birds and vice versa.

In many species, the male differs from the female, or the plumage may vary between the breeding season and the rest of the year. If the bird you have seen was a female, or if, for instance, it was a male in winter plumage, you will still be led to the right answer.

In all cases the abbreviations 'm', 'f', 's' and 'w', or a combination of them, are used when a species is identified. These stand for 'male', 'female', 'summer' and 'winter'. For example, 'BLACKBIRD m' means that the Answer applies to the male blackbird only; the female is quite different. Note that 'summer' and 'winter' are used throughout the book to mean 'during the breeding season' and 'outside the breeding season', rather than any particular months of the year.

In many cases, the sexes are identical – or virtually identical. These are marked 'mf', as for example 'ROBIN mf'. If the sexes are different, but are sufficiently alike to appear under the same Answer, the species is marked 'm-f', as with 'SHELDUCK m-f'.

Similarly 'REED BUNTING mw-f' means that the Answer applies to the male of the species in winter and to the female all year. The male in summer – ms – has an all black head and is therefore dealt with separately.

In the same way 'LITTLE GREBE mfs' means that little grebes of both sexes are identical when in their breeding plumage and that the Answer refers to either of them in summer.

Three columns of potted information are always provided with each Answer to help you make your choice. Let us, for example, take a look at 57. There are four species to choose from and they are set out as follows:

57 (from 55)	**REDSTART** m **STONECHAT** m-f **WHINCHAT** m-f **NUTHATCH** mf	S 14cm EWSi R 12.5cm eWSI S 12.5cm EWSi R 14cm EW

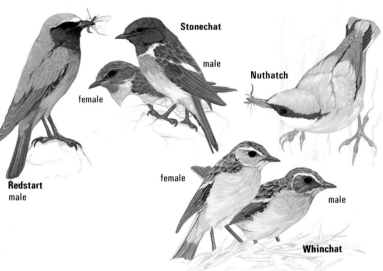

The first column on the right indicates whether the bird is a resident (R) and can therefore be seen all year; or whether it is a summer visitor (S), or a winter visitor (W). So you can tell at once that the stonechat and nuthatch are residents, while the redstart and whinchat may be seen in the breeding season only.

The second column gives the average length of the bird from the tip of its beak to the tip of its tail.

The third column shows its distribution in the British Isles. 'E', 'W', 'S', and 'I' stand for England, Wales, Scotland and Ireland. A capital letter means the species is quite common in a suitable habitat in the country indicated. A small letter means that it occurs there but is scarce.

So you immediately know that the redstart and whinchat are common in England, Wales and Scotland, but rare in Ireland; that the stonechat is rather scarce in England but more often seen in the other three countries; and that the nuthatch occurs quite frequently in England and Wales but is not normally found in Scotland and Ireland.

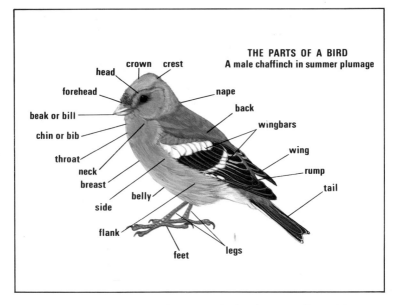

THE PARTS OF A BIRD
A male chaffinch in summer plumage

crown · crest
head
forehead
nape
back
beak or bill
wingbars
chin or bib
wing
throat
rump
neck
breast
tail
belly
side
flank
feet
legs

As you become accustomed to using the book, you will quickly get to know what particular attributes to look for with special care. Obviously the *habitat* is important – the kind of country in which the bird was seen – and so is its *size*. In this book, size is always judged by reference to three species that almost everyone knows. Thus the land-birds are in four size groups:

(a) chaffinch-size or smaller
(b) bigger than chaffinch, not bigger than blackbird
(c) bigger than blackbird, not bigger than rook
(d) bigger than rook.

If you do not already know these three species, they are so common that you should have no difficulty in learning to recognize them very quickly.

A bird's *colour* is also very important, and here you should remember that a great many birds are wholly brown, or wholly brown and white, and you should therefore always look carefully to see if any other colour – including black – can be distinguished.

The shape of the bill can be an important clue to identification, especially with small land birds. Was it thick or thin, straight or curved, long or short? A bird's *voice* is another characteristic that it is often useful to notice, though birdsong is so hard to express in print that I have attempted the task only when it is of vital importance – in distinguishing the chiffchaff from the willow warbler, for example.

When, with experience, you no longer need help with the Questions, you may find it convenient to use the abbreviated key at the very end of the book. This should lead you more quickly to your Answer.

This book does not pretend to be in any way scientific. It does not supply any further information such as nesting habits (except when these are specially helpful for identification). Almost all other bird books arrange the species in families, so that birds of the same ornithological type are considered on the same page. Here the birds grouped in the same Answer are usually those that are most easily confused, though they are often in no way related.

Other bird books may give all or most of the species ever seen in Britain – over 400 of them – though well over half occur extremely seldom. They may even include all those ever seen in Europe. This is admirable if a comprehensive work is required, but difficult for the beginner, who is faced with far more choices than are necessary.

The book ends with an index, in which the 222 species, including those in the supplementary list, appear alphabetically. This is also designed to serve as a checklist, so that you can easily keep a record of every species you have seen. Blank spaces have been left, for any very rare species you may see one day that are not covered by this book.

Good bird-watching!

JK
Killegar
1982

Was it a land bird or a water bird?

In the great majority of cases, the answer will be self-evident. If the bird was swimming or wading, it was certainly a water bird. And it was almost certainly a water bird if it was on the shore (sea, lake or river) or flying low over it; if it was on or near cliffs or flying over the sea; in bushes, reeds or rushes beside water; or on mud-flats.

If it was nowhere near water, it was almost certainly a land bird. In marginal cases, you will come to know by instinct which answer is right.

Some birds, such as gulls, are seen in both these habitats. They will be reached whichever answer is chosen.

Land bird 2   Water bird 166

2   What size was it?

(from 1)

In this book, size is always reckoned by comparing the bird with one of three extremely common species, which almost everyone knows already: the chaffinch (15cm), the blackbird (25cm) and the rook (46cm). Measurements given are from the tip of the bill to the tip of the tail.

Here you have to decide how the bird compares in size with a chaffinch. Birds very close to chaffinch-size will be reached whichever answer is chosen.

Other common birds of much the same size are the robin and the great tit (14cm), the house sparrow and the bullfinch (14.5cm), and the dunnock (15cm).

Chaffinch-size or smaller 3
Bigger than a chaffinch 71

3   What colour was it?

(from 2)

This question refers to the colour of the feathers, ignoring legs and bill.

The plumage of many birds is either brown or brown and white, and they are often among the hardest to identify. So, if a bird seems at first to be entirely brown or brown/white, always look carefully to see if any other colour is present.

If you noticed only brown or brown/white, turn now to 4. Otherwise, *ignore these two colours completely* and decide which other

colour was present or predominant.

For example, birds that are brown/white and red, such as the robin, are found by following 'Red', even though brown/white may have been predominant. Those that are wholly black and white, such as the magpie, are found by following 'Black'.

Note that some species, like the swallow and the cormorant, invariably *look* black, though they are seen, in the hand, to be very dark blue or brown. These too are found by following 'Black'.

Brown or brown/white *only* 4

Ignore brown and white. Choose whichever of these was predominant.
Black 24 Grey 38 Red 49
Yellow/Green 59 Blue 62

 4   # Where was it seen?

(from 3)

'Open country' is the right answer for birds sighted in open fields (perhaps with scattered trees); grassy hill country and rushy wasteland (perhaps overgrown with bushes); heathland, moor and mountain.

   'Not in open country' is correct for

gardens, shrubbery, woodland and forest. Also for all birds seen in towns or cities, or near houses or farm buildings.

In open country 5
Not in open country 16

5   What was the shape of its bill?

(from 4)

All small birds have bills that are quite noticeably either thin and slender or comparatively thick and heavy. The illustration should help you decide.

   The shape of a bird's bill is a useful point of recognition and you should train yourself to look for it, especially with these small brownish birds.

   If you can't make up your mind, follow up the bird under *both* answers, first one and then the other.

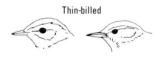
Thin-billed

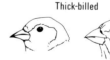
Thick-billed

Thin-billed 6   Thick-billed 13

6   Was it a warbler?

(from 5)

The three possible warblers can be distinguished from all other small, brown, thin-billed birds of the open country because they alone tend to be secretive, almost always inhabiting dense or fairly dense vegetation. They never fly soaring into the sky, nor in rapid direct flight across the

country. The warblers in question are usually, though not always, found in rather moist, rushy land, or in bushy vegetation not far from water.

Yes 7   No 8

SEDGE WARBLER mf   S 13cm EWSI
REED WARBLER mf   S 12.5cm Ew
GRASSHOPPER WARBLER mf   S 13cm EWSI

These three summer visitors are rather inconspicuous and hard to distinguish, apart from their song (see below).

The sedge warbler is noticeably paler than the other two, and has a fairly prominent white eye-stripe running from the base of the bill over the eye to the neck. This eye-stripe is less conspicuous in the grasshopper warbler and almost absent in the reed warbler.

The back and upper wings of the reed warbler are almost plain brown (not streaked with white). Those of the grasshopper warbler are slightly streaked, while the sedge warbler's are quite boldly streaked.

These birds stay so well hidden that they are much more often heard than seen. And their song, though hard to put into words, is easily their most distinctive feature. The reed warbler's is a rather monotonous '*chirruk, chirruk . . . chirr, chirr*'. The sedge warbler's is a rapid intermingling of harsh and sweet notes. The grasshopper warbler's, which is even less like a warble than the song of the other two, is usually compared to the noise made by a fisherman's reel when it is wound in, or by a free-wheeling bicycle.

Sedge Warbler

Grasshopper Warbler

Reed Warbler

(from 6)

8   Did it have noticeable white plumage?

Answer 'No' if the bird was uniformly a speckled brown (apart from whitish underparts). Answer

'Yes' if you noticed white wing-patches or a prominent white rump.

Yes 9   No 10

9   WHEATEAR f   S 14.5cm EWSI
WHINCHAT f   S 12.5cm EWSi

(from 8)

Wheatear female

These two females, which are summer visitors, are quite easily told apart. The wheatear is somewhat bigger; it has a prominent white rump and a T-shaped black and white tail pattern (which may have looked dark brown and white). The whinchat has a streaked back and a white bar on each wing. Both birds have pale eye-stripes.

Note that the male wheatear has a steel-grey back and crown, and conspicuous black markings, which identify him instantly (see 45). The breast of the male whinchat is sufficiently russet to class him under 'Red' (see 57).

Both species belong to the mountain, heathland and hillside. The wheatear is also seen on coastal sand-dunes, the whinchat on scrubby wasteland and rough fields.

Whinchat female

10   Was it a lark or was it a pipit?

(from 8)

The four remaining possible species – two larks and two pipits – are not very easy to distinguish, since they are all extremely plain, brown speckled birds of much the same size. Also, all the males have high-flying song flights, though with important differences.

The two larks are both crested and, though the crests are sometimes inconspicuous to the point of being invisible, they give the heads a generally squarer appearance. The larks also have a noticeably more upright stance, their backs are more boldly striped or speckled, their bills are heavier, and they have more conspicuous pale eye-stripes. The pipits are more slender and have shorter tails.

Lark 11   Pipit 12

SKYLARK mf
WOODLARK mf

R 18cm EWSI
R 15cm Ew

Skylark

Woodlark

The skylark is much the commoner. It is larger, has more of a crest than the woodlark, a rather longer tail, and a white trailing edge to its inner wing. Unlike the skylark, the woodlark prefers the edges of woodland, or country with scattered trees in which it sometimes perches.

Both birds are most often seen when the males are on their spectacular song flights, which also provide the best way of distinguishing them. The skylark flies from the ground almost vertically upwards, singing as he goes. He may then remain hovering for many minutes, sometimes at a great height, pouring forth his song, before descending in silence, again almost vertically.

The woodlark has a circling upward flight and does not hover. His song is briefer than the skylark's and rather more mellow. Unlike the skylark, he sometimes sings when perched.

MEADOW PIPIT mf
TREE PIPIT mf

R 14.5cm EWSI
S 15cm EWS

Meadow Pipit

Tree Pipit

It is extremely hard to distinguish these two unremarkable species except by their song flights and habitats.

The meadow pipit, which is very much more common, usually occurs in treeless country. The tree pipit, which is a summer visitor, is hardly ever seen far from trees.

The song flight of the pipits is much shorter and less spectacular than the larks' and their song is much less impressive. The distinguishing feature is that the meadow pipit invariably rises from the ground, makes a short singing flight and then returns to the ground. The tree pipit almost always rises from a tree, makes his song flight and then returns to a tree – perhaps the same one. Very occasionally, he will land on the ground.

If you can get close enough to see them, the legs of the tree pipit are flesh pink, while those of the meadow pipit are brown. And the meadow pipit has rather more white on the breast.

Did it have prominent white wing-markings?

Answer 'No' if the bird's wings were wholly brown or speckled brown. Answer 'Yes' if you noticed prominent white wing-markings.

Yes 14   No 15

14	**CHAFFINCH** f	R 15cm EWSI
(from 13	**LINNET** f	R 13.5cm EWSI
and 16)	**PIED FLYCATCHER** f	S 13cm EWsi
	SNOW BUNTING m-f	W 16.5cm ewSi

Much the most likely answer is the female chaffinch, one of the most abundant and best known species, with very prominent white wing-bars and a greenish-brown back. For the more distinctive male, see 53.

Next most likely is the female linnet, which is appreciably smaller and has less noticeable wing-bars, a streaked brown back and a brown speckled breast. For the male, which again is more distinctive, see 54.

The male pied flycatcher, handsome and unmistakable, is indeed pied (see 28), but the female isn't. She is a rather greyish-brown above, with almost white underparts and quite noticeable white wing-markings. When perched, she has a way of frequently twitching her tail; her insect-catching routine (see 19) is what often attracts attention.

None of these is liable to be confused with the rarer snow bunting, a winter visitor most often seen in Scotland. In their winter plumage, both sexes are extremely white-looking in general appearance, with almost half-white wings and white underparts. Usually seen on coasts, sometimes in flocks.

For the cirl bunting, which is generally less common except in the south-west, see the supplementary list.

Chaffinch
female

Pied Flycatcher
female

Linnet
female

female

male
(winter)

male
(summer)

Snow Bunting

REED BUNTING mw-f
CORN BUNTING mf
TWITE f

R 15cm EWSI
R 18cm Ewsi
R 13.5cm eSi

female

male
(winter)

Reed Bunting

Corn Bunting

Twite
female

Reed buntings are recognized by their boldly patterned heads. (Note that, in summer, the male has an unmistakable black head, see 34). They are almost always seen in reed beds, except in winter, when they may move to farmland, sometimes close to human dwellings.

The corn bunting is remarkable for being so unremarkable: it is a uniform streaky brown. Rather larger than a chaffinch, it is heavy looking and plumpish with a short, powerful beak, and it usually flies with its legs dangling. Its song, which is its most distinctive feature, sounds like the jangle of a bunch of keys. Corn buntings are by no means confined to cornfields, and often sing from fence posts or telephone wires.

The female twite is also undistinguished in appearance, but is noticeably smaller and has indistinct pale wing-markings. (Note that the male twite has a pink rump, see 58). Mainly a bird of the uplands, especially in summertime.

Did it have prominent white wing-markings?
(from 4)

Answer 'Yes' if you noticed prominent white wing-markings. Answer 'No' if the bird's wings were wholly brown or speckled brown.

Yes 14 No 17

Was it a warbler?
(from 16)

The three possible warblers, which are summer visitors, can be told from the five other species still 'left in the hunt' because they are comparatively shy birds. They are not very often clearly seen as they flit through the trees or undergrowth, though their voices may fill the land. Even the male in song usually chooses a secret, leaf-hidden perch.

Yes 18 No 19

GARDEN WARBLER mf	S 14cm EWsi
BLACKCAP f	R 14cm EWsi
WHITETHROAT f	S 14cm EWSI

The garden warbler is the most likely of these because the two others, being females, do not sing and are therefore even less noticeable. It is an absolutely plain brown bird with a whiter breast, distinguished only by the male's glorious bursts of song.

The female blackcap is recognized at once by her misleading chestnut cap. For the more conspicuous male, whose cap is indeed black, see 34.

The female whitethroat has, as might be expected, a white throat. The male bird, which is also white-throated, has a grey head and nape (see 40). Note that the lesser whitethroat, which is only fractionally smaller, is altogether greyer (see 46).

All three normally visit us only in the breeding season, but the blackcap sometimes stays the winter, especially in Ireland and south-west England.

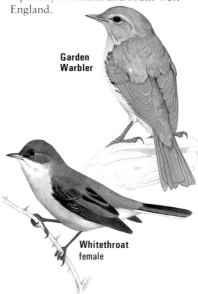

Garden Warbler

Blackcap
female

Whitethroat
female

19

Was it a flycatcher?

Flycatchers, which are summer visitors, can be distinguished from all other birds because – in direct contrast to the warblers – they like to choose a prominent perch, such as a gatepost or a railing, from which they make repeated short flights in search of insects, often twisting almost vertically upwards.

Flycatchers

Yes 20 No 21

20   SPOTTED FLYCATCHER mf   S 14cm EWSI

(from 19)

The spotted flycatcher is
misleadingly named because it isn't
the least bit spotted. It is a rather
plain, all brown bird, with a streaked
breast and head, and might well
escape notice altogether but for its
conspicuous insect-catching routine
(see 19).

    Often twitches its tail when
perched.

**Spotted
Flycatcher**

21   Was it a house sparrow?

(from 19)

The house sparrow is so abundantly
common and universally known that
your choice of reply should pose no
problem; but see 22 for more details
if necessary.

Yes 22   No 23

22   HOUSE SPARROW f   R 14.5cm EWSI

(from 21)

The male bird (see 36) has noticeable
black and grey plumage, but the
female is wholly brown and white,
with streaked back and unstreaked
breast, a pale eye-stripe and paler
wing-bars. A friend of man, this
highly gregarious species is usually
found in cities, towns and villages; it
is generally seen on farms, but may
not appear at all over tracts of open
country. Note the heavy bill.

House Sparrow
female

23   WREN mf   R 9.5cm EWSI
TREECREEPER mf   R 12.5cm EWSI

(from 21)

These two little birds are very easy to
tell apart, if only because the
treecreeper – who seldom leaves
woodland – seems indeed to spend its
entire life creeping up trees, usually
hardwoods, in search of insects, then

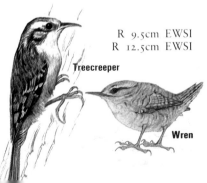

Treecreeper

Wren

fluttering to near ground level and starting all over again – a monotonous existence.

The well-loved wren, with its barred warm-brown plumage and paler underparts, is sometimes seen perched, when its short cocked-up tail becomes a trademark. More often it is noticed in its whirring, low-level flight through shrubs or undergrowth. Its song is loud for its size, and sweetly wistful.

The treecreeper, alone among small birds, has a longish curved bill; it also has a noticeable white breast and eye-stripe.

24 Was it mainly (or wholly) black and white?

(from 3)

Answer 'Yes' even though the white areas may not have been very extensive; and though a small area of some other colour (especially red) may have been noticed.

Yes 25   No 29

25 Was it a swallow or swallow-like?

(from 24)

Swallows and swallow-like birds are summer visitors with very long wings and forked tails. They are almost always seen in flight, which is rapid and joyous. The swift is not a swallow, but is included here because it certainly is swallow-like and is often confused with members of the swallow family.

Yes 89   No 26

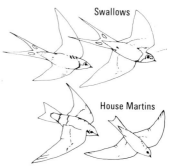

Swallows

House Martins

26 Did it have a long tail?

(from 25)

Answer 'Yes' only if the tail was about half the entire length of the bird.

Yes 27   No 28

27

(from 26 and 49)

LONG-TAILED TIT mf
PIED WAGTAIL m-f s-w

R 14cm EWSI
R 18cm EWSI

There is no danger of confusing these two very different species. The long-tailed tit is very small indeed: without its spoon-handle of a tail – more than half its total length – it would be the smallest British bird.

Long-tailed Tit

winter

summer

Pied Wagtail

Mainly black and white, but with a pinkish tinge to its back and belly, it is most often seen flitting restlessly through the branches of small trees or bushes, sometimes in small flocks.

The pied wagtail, which is much more common, is usually seen on the ground, often near water or human habitation. It does indeed constantly wag its tail. Its plumage varies with sex, season and age, but is always a combination of black and/or slate grey with white.

Both birds have undulating flights.

28	**BLACK REDSTART** m	R 14cm Ewi
	PIED FLYCATCHER m	S 13cm EWsi
(from 26)	**LESSER SPOTTED WOODPECKER** m-f	R 14.5cm EW

As the illustrations show, these three handsome birds have marked distinguishing features. The male black redstart is mainly black, with some white on the wings and underparts, but is distinguished from all other black and white species by his conspicuous red tail. The female has the same red tail but is mainly brown/grey (see 48). Sometimes seen in cities, including London.

The male pied flycatcher is wholly black and white – the most boldly pied small bird of the region. He is always very conspicuous when perched on a fence or gatepost for frequent brief insect-catching sorties. The female (see 14) is similar but brown and white.

The lesser spotted woodpecker is almost always confined to woodland. Both sexes have a black-and-white barred back. The male alone has a distinctive red crown. This woodpecker is distinguished from all others by its very small size (much

Lesser Spotted Woodpecker

female

male

Black Redstart male

Pied Flycatcher male

the same as a chaffinch). All others are blackbird-size or larger.

The flycatchers are summer visitors. So usually is the black redstart, but a few birds stay for the winter. All woodpeckers are resident.

29 Was the black plumage confined to the head?

(from 24)

This question needs no elaboration.   Yes 30   No 35

30 Was it a member of the tit family?

(from 29)

Members of the tit family are instantly recognized, once you get to know them, by their small size, rather rounded shape and acrobatic skills. Of an active and restless nature, they prefer woodland, but are friends of man and will gladly visit bird tables and nesting boxes.

Yes 31   No 32

Tits

31
COAL TIT mf
MARSH TIT mf
WILLOW TIT mf

(from 30)

R 11.5cm EWSI
R 11.5cm EWs
R 11.5cm EWs

The great tit and blue tit have black markings, but their breasts are such a bright yellow that black could hardly have been thought their predominant colour and they are listed under 'Yellow' – see 62.

The coal tit is distinguished from the marsh tit and willow tit by its slate-grey back (not brown) and from all other tits by the quite prominent white patch on its nape.

The marsh and willow tits both have black crowns and white cheeks like the coal tit, but their backs are brown and they have black bibs. They are very hard to tell apart. The main difference is that the willow tit's black bib is very slightly larger. Also, but less noticeably, its crown is a glossier black.

Coal Tit

Willow Tit

Marsh Tit

Their calls, if heard, are probably the best way to distinguish them. The marsh tit's is usually written '*pitchu*', the willow tit's a monosyllabic '*chay*'. The latter also has a very occasional song, which is rather like a warbler's.

Despite their names, neither has a special liking for marshes or willows.

32 Did it have a reddish-coloured breast?

(from 30)

This question needs no elaboration.

Yes 33 No 34

33 STONECHAT m

R 13cm eWSI

(from 32)

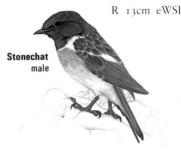

Stonechat
male

The male stonechat is the only bird of the region with a wholly black head, prominent white collar and chestnut breast. The female (see 57) has a speckly brown head, no collar and a paler breast. Both sexes show white wing-markings.

Stonechats are almost exclusively birds of the heathland, hills and mountains, except in winter when they may visit farmland.

34 REED BUNTING ms
BLACKCAP m

R 15cm EWSI
R 14cm EWsi

(from 32)

The male reed bunting is unmistakable in summer with his black head, white collar and 'moustache', boldly marked back and wings, whitish breast and underparts. He is almost always found in reed beds, except in winter when he may appear on farmland. At that time of year, his head becomes dark brown and he closely resembles the female (see 15).

The male blackcap, which is a warbler, is also easy to recognize – from his black cap, grey-brown back and paler underparts. But he lives in woodland or shrubbery, often with thick undergrowth and, though less secretive than many warblers, is much more frequently heard than seen. He sings in fine bursts of song. The female resembles the male but has a chestnut cap (see 18).

Though mainly a summer visitor, the blackcap sometimes winters here.

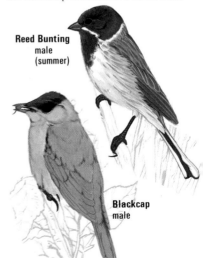

Reed Bunting
male
(summer)

Blackcap
male

Was it a member of the sparrow family?

(from 29)
You must surely already know the house sparrow, and the only other member of the family closely resembles it. Note that the dunnock, though also known as the hedge sparrow, is not a member of the sparrow family (see 47).

Yes 36   No 37

| 36 | **HOUSE SPARROW** m
TREE SPARROW mf |

(from 35)

R 14.5cm EWSI
R 14cm Ewsi

The male house sparrow has a grey crown and black bib. The female is plainer (see 22). The tree sparrow (sexes alike) has a chestnut crown, a smaller black bib and a black spot on each cheek.

The habitats of these two species will usually distinguish them. The highly gregarious house sparrow is generally found wherever there are people, even in the busiest cities. The much less common tree sparrow is mainly a bird of the open woodland or of shrubby undergrowth, some

Tree Sparrow

House Sparrow
male

distance from human habitation; but it is sometimes found in gardens.

| 37 | **WHEATEAR** m-f |

(from 35 and 79)

S 14.5cm EWSI

The steel-grey back and crown of the male wheatear is even more noticeable than the black plumage on his cheeks, wings and tail. The female is mainly brown/white but, like the male, has a T-shaped black and white tail pattern. Both sexes have pale eye-stripes and conspicuous white rumps.

A summer visitor, the wheatear is a bird of heathland, hillside and mountain. It also visits coastal sand dunes.

male

female

Wheatear

| 38 | Did it have a long tail?

(from 3)
Answer 'Yes' if the tail constituted almost half the total length of the bird.

Yes 97   No 39

(from 38)

Choose carefully from these five options the part or parts of the body where the grey plumage was noticeable.

Head only [40] Back only [41]
Crown and back [42] Head and breast [47] Generally grey [48]

 LINNET ms-mw
WHITETHROAT m

(from 39)

R 13.5cm EWSI
S 14cm EWSI

These two very different species have only their grey heads in common.

The male linnet, found mostly in open country, is distinguished in summer by his red forehead and breast. These are less marked in winter but still present. He is mainly brown, with a grey head, white wing-bar and white underside. The female has no grey or red plumage (see 14).

The male whitethroat, a summer visitor like all warblers, has a fairly prominent white throat, a grey head and pale underparts. Otherwise he is brownish: the wings are rather a reddish brown, the back a rather greyish brown. Again the female has no grey plumage (see 18). The lesser whitethroat is similar, but has more extensive grey areas (see 46).

Linnet
male

Whitethroat
male

The whitethroat likes hedgerows, rough scrubby undergrowth and occasionally gardens.

41 **BULLFINCH** m-f
BLACKCAP m-f

(from 39)

R 15cm EWSI
R 14cm EWSi

These two species cannot be confused. The male bullfinch is extremely handsome: bright red breast and cheeks, grey back, black crown, black wingtips and tail. The female is a toned-down version of the male – pinkish brown where he is red, dark brown where he is grey. Despite these bright colours, the white rump of both sexes is often the most noticeable feature, if the bird is

seen briefly as it flies away into hedgerow or undergrowth. Usually occurs in orchards, gardens, woodland and shrubbery.

Blackcaps are very different: they are thin-billed, their backs are rather a brownish grey, their breasts and underparts pale. It is only the male whose cap is black; the female's is chestnut. Blackcaps tend to be rather secretive, though less than most

Bullfinch

Blackcap

other warblers, especially when the male is singing. They generally stay in the cover of young trees and bushes.

Blackcaps are normally summer visitors, but a few birds stay the winter.

Did it have a red or reddish breast?

(from 39)
Answer 'Yes' if you noticed any degree of redness in the bird's breast.

Yes 43 No 44

REDSTART m
NUTHATCH mf
(from 42)

S 14cm EWSi
R 14cm EW

These two conspicuous species cannot possibly be confused. The male redstart, a summer visitor, stands out with his grey crown and back, white forehead, black throat, red breast and tail. The female is much plainer (see 58).

The nuthatch has a lighter grey crown and back, a paler reddish breast and a black eye-stripe, and is the only small bird with such a long straight bill.

Both species have similar habitats: they like woodland, parks and gardens. The nuthatch, which will visit bird tables, spends much of its time looking for insects in the bark of trees. It is an expert acrobat and is the only bird that can creep down trees head first. The redstart catches

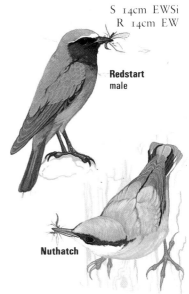

Redstart
male

Nuthatch

insects on short flights up and down from a perch.

(from 42)

'Open country' is the right answer for birds seen in moorland, heath, mountainy country and downs, usually treeless or nearly so.

'Not in open country' is correct for hedgerows, woodland, rough scrubby undergrowth, parks and gardens.

In open country 45
Not in open country 46

45 WHEATEAR m

S 14.5cm EWSI

(from 44 and 92)

The male wheatear is very conspicuous, with his steel-grey crown and back, prominent white rump, black wings and tail, and a black patch through and behind the eye. A summer visitor, he is a bird of the mountain and moorland, though also found in grassy hill country and on sand dunes. The female is much less distinctive (see 37).

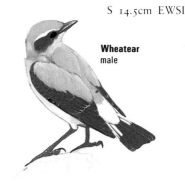

Wheatear
male

46 WHITETHROAT m
LESSER WHITETHROAT mf

S 14cm EWSI
S 13.5cm Ews

(from 44)

These two species, like all warblers, are summer visitors. They are not easy to tell apart. The lesser whitethroat is very slightly smaller because of its rather shorter tail, and has a dark patch around the eye which, however, is not very noticeable. Its legs are pale brown, while the whitethroat's are black-looking.

Both species do indeed have white throats. The head and back of the male whitethroat are a rather brownish grey; those of the lesser whitethroat (sexes alike) are greyer, and so are its wings.

Note that the female whitethroat has no grey plumage (see 18).

The main difference between the two birds is in their song. The

Whitethroat
male

Lesser Whitethroat

whitethroat sings in quick, high-pitched bursts; the lesser whitethroat produces an unmelodious rattle, sometimes preceded by a subdued warble. Both males occasionally make short, low-flying song flights.

47   DUNNOCK mf
(from 39)

R 14.5cm EWSI

The dunnock, otherwise known (wrongly) as the hedge sparrow, is the only bird of the region with a grey head and breast. Note the slender bill, which is quite unlike the heavy bill of the sparrows.

Found almost everywhere if some cover is available.

Dunnock

48   BLACK REDSTART f
(from 39)

R 14cm Ewi

The female black redstart is the only bird of the region that is generally grey but with a bright chestnut tail. The male is rather handsomer (see 28). Inhabits towns and cities, including London, as well as rocky mountainsides.

**Black Redstart
female**

Primarily a summer visitor, but is sometimes seen in winter.

49   Did it have an extremely long tail?
(from 3)

Answer 'Yes' if the tail made up over half the total length of the bird.   Yes 27 No 50

50   Did it have a red breast?
(from 49)

Answer 'Yes' if all or any of the red plumage you noticed was on the breast.   Yes 51 No 58

51   Did the red plumage extend to the head?
(from 50)

Answer 'Yes' if there was any red plumage on the head as well as the breast.   Yes 52 No 55

(from 51)
Let us begin by eliminating these two extremely common birds, which almost everyone knows already. If you don't, look first at 53 before going on to 54.

Yes 53   No 54

53   ROBIN mf   R 14cm EWSI
CHAFFINCH m   R 15cm EWSI

(from 52)

Robin

Chaffinch
male

Both species are unafraid of man and are often seen near human habitations.

The robin is the only bird to combine such a conspicuous red breast, throat and cheeks with otherwise all-brown plumage (apart from the whitish underparts).

The red plumage of the male chaffinch extends over much the same areas but is more of a reddish brown. He is at once distinguished by his blue-grey crown and nape, which are duller in winter, his greenish-brown back, his heavy bill, and his very noticeable white wing-markings.

Note that the female chaffinch is altogether plainer and has no red plumage (see 14).

54   BULLFINCH m-f   R 15cm EWSI
LINNET ms-mw   R 13.5cm EWSI
(from 52)
REDPOLL ms   R 13cm EWSI
CROSSBILL m   R 16.5cm ewSi

Bullfinches are extremely handsome, especially the male, with his bright red breast and cheeks, grey back, black wing-tips and tail. The female is similar, but less colourful: pinkish brown where the male is red, dark brown where he is grey. Both sexes have a white rump which, despite their gaudy colours, is often the most noticeable feature if the bird is glimpsed as it flies away.

The male linnet in summer has a red breast and forehead; these are less marked in winter but still present. It is mainly a bird of the open country, mostly brown in colour, with a grey head, white wing-bar and pale underparts. The female has no red or grey plumage (see 14).

The male redpoll in summer has a similar red breast and forehead, but is distinguished by his black chin and

male

female

Bullfinch

Linnet male

Crossbill male

Redpoll male (summer)

the absence of grey plumage. His red rump may also be noticed. In winter his breast and rump lose their redness and he looks like the female (see 58).

The male crossbill is at once distinguished by his almost all-red colouring: he is the reddest-looking bird of the region. His wings and tail are darker. Usually seen in conifers, often high up in the trees and frequently in small flocks. The crossed bill is not very noticeable.

The female is green (see 67), so if you saw red birds and green birds in company, they are certain to have been crossbills.

55 Did the red plumage extend to the tail or wings?

(from 51)

Answer 'Yes' if you noticed red plumage on the tail or wings as well as on the breast. Answer 'No' if it

was confined to the breast.

Yes 56 No 57

56

(from 55)

REDSTART m
BRAMBLING ms-mw-f

S 14cm EWSi
W 14.5cm EWSi

Redstart male

female

male (summer)

male (winter)

Brambling

The male redstart, a summer visitor, is instantly recognized by his red breast and tail, his grey crown and back, white forehead and black throat – a most striking combination. The female is also red-tailed but otherwise mainly greyish brown.

The male brambling in summer has an unmistakable black head and back but, because he is a winter visitor, is seldom seen here in this finery. The black areas turn brown in winter, when he looks very like the female. In both sexes, the redness of the breast extends to the shoulders, and both have white rumps. Usually seen in parks, fields and gardens, often in flocks with other finches.

(from 55)

57	**REDSTART** m	S 14cm EWSi
	STONECHAT m-f	R 12.5cm eWSI
(from 55)	**WHINCHAT** m-f	S 12.5cm EWSi
	NUTHATCH mf	R 14cm EW

Stonechat male

Nuthatch

female

Redstart male

female

male

Whinchat

The male redstart appears here in case you missed his red tail (see 56).

The breasts of the other species listed, especially the whinchat, are not conspicuously red, but have a russet or chestnut colouring that justifies their inclusion here.

The male stonechat is the only bird of the region with a wholly black head, prominent white collar and chestnut breast. The female has a speckly brown head, no collar and a paler breast. Both sexes show white wing-markings.

The whinchats are well marked birds, with pale eye-stripes, streaked backs, and white wing-bars. The sexes are very similar, but the male's plumage is somewhat darker and his breast more tinged with red. Whinchats are summer visitors.

The nuthatch cannot be confused with any of the foregoing – or indeed with any other species. It has a light grey crown and back, a very pale red breast, a black eye-stripe and is the only small bird with such a long straight bill.

Moreover stonechats and whinchats are birds of the mountain and moorland, or of grassy uplands and scrubby wasteland. The nuthatch, an expert acrobat, is the only bird that can creep down trees head first in its search for insects. It prefers woodland, parks and gardens.

BLACK REDSTART m-f R 14cm Ewi
REDSTART f S 14cm EWSi
REDPOLL mw-f R 13cm EWSI
TWITE m R 13.5cm eSi

female
male
Twite
male

Black Redstart

Redstart
female

female
male

Redpoll

The red plumage of the black redstart (both sexes) and redstart (female only) is confined to the tail. The male redstart has a reddish breast as well (see 56).

The male black redstart is otherwise mainly sooty black, with some white on his wings and underparts. The female is much greyer. Black redstarts are usually summer visitors, but a few pairs stay the winter.

The female redstart is similar to the female black redstart but is more of a brownish grey. She is exclusively a summer visitor.

The female redpoll's red plumage is only on her forehead – and so is the male's in winter. In summer, he has a red breast as well (see 54). Their black chins distinguish the redpolls from all other species. Note that, apart from these two constant features, their size and colour are liable to variation.

The red plumage of the twite is confined to the rump and is not very noticeable. It is absent in the female

(see 15). Both sexes have pale wing-bars but are generally rather undistinguished unless you happen to notice the male's red rump.

The twite is a bird of the open country, preferring mountain and moorland in summer, often descending to open fields in winter. The redstart and redpoll prefer woodland, gardens, shrubbery and parks. The black redstart is a bird of the rocky mountainside, but is also at home in towns and villages, and even in London.

59 Was it extremely small?

(from 3)
Answer 'Yes' only if it was a mere
9cm in length.

Yes ⌷60⌷ No ⌷61⌷

60 GOLDCREST m-f

R 9cm EWSI

(from 59)

The goldcrest is tiny – the smallest
British bird. It is a delight to watch as
it flits restlessly – sometimes in flocks
– from branch to branch in
woodland, often coniferous. It has
whitish underparts, but is
distinguished by its generally
greenish-brown colouring and in
particular by its crown. This
provides the only way of
distinguishing between the sexes: the
male's is yellow and orange, the

female
male
Goldcrest

female's yellow only, in both cases
edged with black.

61 Was it a member of the tit family?

(from 59)
Members of the tit family are
instantly recognized, once you get to
know them, by their small size,
rather rounded shape, acrobatic
skills and, in many cases, bright
colouring. Of an active and restless
nature, they are often seen in
woodland, but are friends of man
and will gladly visit bird tables or use
nesting boxes.

Yes ⌷62⌷ No ⌷63⌷

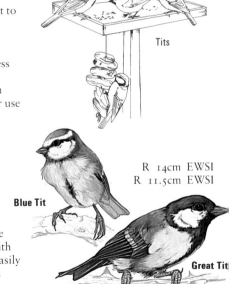

Tits

62 GREAT TIT mf
   BLUE TIT mf

R 14cm EWSI
R 11.5cm EWSI

(from 3
and 61)

These two delightful birds are the
only members of the tit family with
bright yellow breasts. They are easily
told apart. The great tit, which is

Blue Tit

Great Tit

appreciably larger, has a black cap and throat, with a black stripe down the centre of its breast. The blue has a blue cap, wings and tail; it is the only land bird with such extensive genuinely blue plumage.

The great tit is sometimes confused with the coal tit (see 31), but the latter is noticeably smaller and has no yellow breast.

63 Was it a warbler?

(from 61)

The warblers are small, thin-billed birds. They tend to be secretive, staying almost always in dense or fairly dense cover. The only three yellowish species are usually confined to shrubs and light woodland, through which they move actively and restlessly. They seldom show themselves for long, though the males will occasionally when they are singing.

Yes 64 No 65

64

CHIFFCHAFF mf	S 11cm EWSI
WILLOW WARBLER mf	S 11cm EWSI
WOOD WARBLER mf	S 12.5cm EWS

(from 63)

All three are summer visitors. The chiffchaff and the willow warbler are virtually identical, apart from their very distinctive songs (see below). Both have greenish brown upperparts, yellowish breasts and a pale streak through the eye. The chiffchaff may have rather darker legs, but these are not at all noticeable.

The rather larger wood warbler is similar to both, but has a yellower breast, face and eye-stripe, and much whiter underparts. It usually occurs higher up in trees than the two others.

Their identifying songs are, as always, hard to put into words. The chiffchaff repeats his own name – 'chiff . . . chaff . . . chiff . . . chaff' – endlessly and monotonously, on almost the same note. The willow warbler is absolutely different: in bursts of five to six seconds, he pours out a wistful stream of slowly descending notes. The wood warbler's song is less noticeable but distinctive: a prolonged, quavering trill.

Chiffchaff

Wood Warbler

Willow Warbler

(from 63)

65   Did it have a long tail?

(from 63)

Answer 'Yes' if the tail made up
almost half the total length.   Yes 191 No 66

66   Did it show green plumage?

(from 65)

Answer 'Yes' if you noticed green
plumage, with or without any
yellow.   Yes 67 No 68

67   GREENFINCH m-f   R 14.5cm EWSI
          CROSSBILL f   R 16.5cm ewSi

(from 66)

Greenfinch

female

male

**Crossbill
female**

The greenfinch (both sexes) and the
female crossbill are the only small
birds showing extensive green
plumage.

    For the female crossbill, which is
very much the rarer and noticeably
larger, turn to 108 for description.

The greenfinch likes quite open
country, fields with scattered trees,
or shrubbery, parks, gardens and
hedgerows. The female is browner
than the male and is less well
marked. Both sexes have yellow wing
patches.

68   Did it have a bright red face?

(from 66)

This question needs no elaboration.   Yes 69 No 70

69   GOLDFINCH mf   R 12cm EWSI

(from 68)

The multicoloured goldfinch cannot
be mistaken for any other species. Its

red/white/black head is immediately
distinctive. It also has a black tail and

wings, with broad, bright yellow wing-bars which are extremely conspicuous, especially in flight. By contrast the white rump is less important.

The goldfinch likes shrubbery, parks and gardens, or sometimes open fields with scattered trees. It often feeds on thistles.

Goldfinch

70	**YELLOWHAMMER** m-f	R 16.5cm EWSI
	SISKIN m-f	R 12cm ewSI

(from 68)

The yellowhammer is a bird of the fields and hedgerows, of woodland margins and clearings. It is the only species that gives the general appearance of being wholly brown and yellow. The male has a bright yellow head, boldly marked with brown, and a yellow/brown breast and underparts. The female is a toned down version of the male.

The male siskin, which is much smaller, differs from all other birds in having a black crown and chin to set off his yellow face and breast. The female's head has no black plumage and she is much less yellow.

Siskins are mainly birds of the woodland, but in winter they may venture into shrubby country with small trees, especially alders, or even into parks and gardens.

male

female

Yellowhammer

male

female

Siskin

| 71 |

What size was it?

(from 2)
You have decided that it was larger than a chaffinch. Now you have to make up your mind if it was also larger than another very well-known species, the blackbird (25cm). Birds very close to blackbird-size will be reached whichever answer is chosen.

Other common birds that are close to blackbird-size are the song thrush (23cm) and the mistle thrush (27cm).

Blackbird-size or smaller [72]
Larger than a blackbird [109]

(from 71)

This question refers only to the colour of the feathers; it ignores the legs and bill.

The plumage of many birds is either brown or brown and white – and these are often among the hardest to identify. So, if a bird seems at first to be entirely brown or brown/white, always look carefully to see if any other colour is present.

If you noticed only brown or brown/white, turn now to 73. Otherwise, ignore these two colours completely and decide what other colour was present or predominant.

For example, birds that are brown/white and red, such as the robin, are found by following 'Red',

even though brown/white may have been predominant. Those that are wholly black and white, such as the magpie, are found by following 'Black'.

Note that some species invariably *look* black, though they are seen, in the hand, to be very dark blue or brown. The swallow and cormorant are examples. These too are found by following 'Black'.

Brown or brown/white only 73
Ignore brown and white. Choose which of the following was predominant.
Black 88 Grey 96 Red 101
Yellow 106 Green 108

73 Was it a member of the owl family?

(from 72)

Owls are almost always instantly recognized as such from their large heads, large eyes, flattened faces, short hooked beaks and powerful claws. They cannot move their eyes independently of their heads, so must turn their whole head to look around. Owls fly absolutely silently, usually at dusk or at night.

Yes 74 No 75

Owls

Little Owl

R 22cm EWs

74 LITTLE OWL mt

(from 73 and 127)

If it was an owl, it must have been a little owl, the only member of the family in this region that is blackbird-size or smaller. This species is less nocturnal than the others, and may be seen in daytime perched on a post or other lookout,

usually bobbing its head. It likes open country with scattered trees, but is often seen near houses.

For the larger owls, see 128.

75 Was it a member of the snipe family?

(from 73)

Snipe

Members of the snipe family can be distinguished at once by their long thin bills and rapid flight – they are hardly ever seen at rest. Snipe are almost always found in wet, marshy ground, but they also visit dry heathland and mountain, which justifies their inclusion among land birds.

Yes 76   No 77

76 SNIPE mf
JACK SNIPE mf

(from 75)

R 27cm EWSI
W 19cm EWSI

These two species are very similar in appearance and habitat, but are quite easy to distinguish. The smaller jack snipe flies in an almost straight line when disturbed, whereas the snipe flies in a zigzag. Also, the jack snipe doesn't fly nearly as far before settling again in the heather or bogland, whereas the snipe usually flies out of sight.

The jack snipe, a winter visitor, is usually less common. Its bill is shorter than the snipe's and it is rather darker brown.

Snipe

Jack Snipe

77 What size was it?

(from 75)

You have decided that it was larger than a chaffinch (15cm) but not larger than a blackbird (25cm). Now you have to consider if it was closer to chaffinch-size or blackbird-size.

The remaining possible species are all quite noticeably either one or the other.

Nearer to chaffinch 78
Nearer to blackbird 86

78 Where was it seen?

(from 77)

'Open country' is the right answer for birds seen in open fields, perhaps with scattered trees, grassy hill country, and rushy wasteland overgrown with bushes, heathland, moor and mountain.

'Not in open country' is correct for hedgerows, shrubbery, woodland, parks and gardens.

Open country 79
Not in open country 85

Did it have a conspicuous white rump?

(from 78)

Answer 'Yes' if you noticed that the bird had a conspicuous white rump (and, less noticeably, a black/white tail pattern) as it flew away from you, probably over mountain land or heather.

Yes 37 No 80

Was it very secretive?

(from 79)

Answer 'Yes' if the bird was hidden in long grass, standing corn or vegetation, and broke cover only when you came close to it.

Yes 81 No 82

QUAIL f

S 18cm ewsi

(from 80)

**Quail
female**

Quail are plump and rounded. The female is entirely brown and white, while the male has a black patch on his throat (see 94). Both sexes have striped heads, but the female's is less well marked. They are very reluctant to break cover; when they do, they fly low with rapid wing-beats. An uncommon summer visitor.

What was the shape of its bill?

(from 80)

All smallish birds have bills that are quite noticeably either thin and slender or comparatively thick and heavy. The illustration should help you to decide.

The shape of a bird's bill is a useful point of recognition and you should train yourself to look for it, especially with these brownish birds. If you can't make up your mind, follow up the bird under both answers, first one and then the other.

Thin-billed

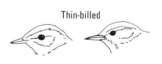

Thick-billed

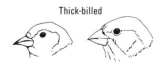

Thin-billed 83 Thick-billed 84

(from 82)

The four remaining possible species – two larks and two pipits – are not very easy to tell apart, since they are all extremely plain, brown speckled birds of much the same size. And all the males have high-flying song flights, though with important differences.

The two larks are both crested and, though the crests are sometimes inconspicuous to the point of being invisible, they give the heads a generally squarer appearance. The larks also have a more noticeably upright stance, their backs are more boldly striped or speckled, their bills are heavier, and they have more conspicuous pale eye-stripes. The pipits are more slender and have shorter tails.

Larks 11 Pipits 12

84

REED BUNTING mw-f
CORN BUNTING mf
SNOW BUNTING m-f

(from 82)

R 15cm EWSI
R 18cm EwSi
W 16.5cm ewSi

Reed Bunting

female

male (winter)

Corn Bunting

male (winter)

female

Snow Bunting

male (summer)

Reed buntings are recognized by their boldly patterned heads. (Note that, in summer, the male has an unmistakable black head, see 94.) They are almost always seen in reed beds, except in winter when they may move to farmland, sometimes quite close to human dwellings.

The corn bunting, by no means found only in cornfields, is remarkable for being so unremarkable. It is a uniform streaky brown, heavy-looking and plumpish with a short powerful beak, and it usually flies with legs dangling. Its song is its most distinctive feature. Often given from a fence post or telephone wire, it sounds like the jangling of a bunch of keys.

Neither of these is liable to be confused with the snow buntings, which are winter visitors most often seen in Scotland. In their winter plumage, these handsome little birds are extremely white-looking, with almost half-white wings and white breasts and undersides. Usually seen on coasts, sometimes in flocks.

NIGHTINGALE mf   S 16.5cm Ew

Nightingale

The secretive nightingale, a summer visitor, keeps well hidden in shrubs and bushes, often where the ground is moist. It is therefore much more often heard than seen. Its plumage is undistinguished – brown with whitish underparts and a rather chestnut tail – but its liquid song, of infinite variety, is glorious. The nightingale is usually heard at night, but also sings during the day.

86 Was it a member of the thrush family?

(from 77)

The thrush and blackbird are well-known to almost everyone. All other members of the family are very like them, and easily recognizable. They are much the same size and shape, square-tailed, thin-billed, and usually fine singers.

Thrushes

Yes 87 No 129

87
(from 86 and 125)

BLACKBIRD f   R 25cm EWSI
SONG THRUSH mf   R 23cm EWSI
MISTLE THRUSH mf   R 27cm EWSI
RING OUZEL f   S 24cm EWSi

The female blackbird is something like the male, but she is dark brown instead of black and her bill is not so yellow. (For the male bird, see 91.) Her breast has very few spots or speckles.

The song thrush and the mistle thrush are rather alike in appearance. They are a much lighter brown and very definitely spotted – especially the latter. The mistle thrush, which is noticeably larger, has more of a grey-brown back, spots that continue from the breast and throat right up into the cheeks, and white outer tail feathers. Also the mistle thrush is more a bird of the open country, though also seen in gardens, parks and woodland. It may fly high above the fields, with a characteristic rattling flight-call, to lodge in the topmost branches of a high tree.

The female ring ouzel is easily distinguished from the others. A summer visitor, she is exclusively a bird of the moorland and mountain. Furthermore, she has a noticeable white crescent on her speckly brown breast. The male bird is black save for a prominent white crescent (see 93).

Note that the fieldfare and the

redwing, which arrive in flocks in winter, are much like other thrushes, and are mainly brownish, but the former is listed among birds showing grey (see 100) and the latter among birds showing red (see 104).

Song Thrush

Blackbird
female

Mistle Thrush

Ring Ouzel
female

88 Was it a swallow or swallow-like?

(from 72)

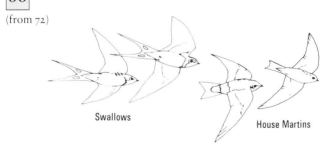

Swallows

House Martins

Swallows and swallow-like birds, which most people can recognize as such, are summer visitors with very long wings and forked tails. They are almost always seen in flight, which is rapid and joyous.

The swift is not a swallow, but is included here because it certainly is swallow-like and is often confused with members of the swallow family.

Yes 89 No 90

SWALLOW mf   S 19cm EWSI
HOUSE MARTIN mf   S 12.5cm EWSI
SWIFT mf   S 16.5cm EWSI

Swallow

House Martin

Swift

These three summer visitors are often wrongly identified by beginners but are really not hard to tell apart.

The red throat of the swallow is very seldom noticed. What really distinguishes it are its very long tail streamers, clearly visible as it passes overhead or wheels in the sunshine. (Note, however, that this year's young birds do not yet possess these streamers; they have short tails like the house martin's.)

The house martin, which is substantially smaller, is equally easy to recognize – from its conspicuous white rump, hard to miss between back and tail as it soars away from you. Both species have white underparts.

The swift, smaller than the swallow in length but not in wing span, appears all black apart from its white chin, and has a stiffer, more direct flight than the swallow's, with a faster, more regular wing-beat. Though also seen in open country, it is much more a bird of towns and villages than the others, where it flies screeching above the rooftops.

The nesting habits of these species provide an important clue to recognition. It is the house martin that builds under the eaves of houses. The swallow constructs an open nest, on a beam or ledge, almost always inside a building, usually a farm outhouse. The swift prefers a chimney or hollow tree.

Note that the swift, in the hand, is seen to be very dark brown rather than black, while the swallow and martin are very dark blue. But all three seem rather to be black and are therefore dealt with here.

90   Was it wholly black?

(from 88)

Answer 'Yes' if the bird's plumage was either entirely black, or black with a greenish/purplish sheen.

Yes 91   No 92

BLACKBIRD m
STARLING mfs-mfw

R 25cm EWSI
R 21.5cm EWSI

(from 90
and 139)

The male blackbird is well known to almost everyone – the only jet black bird with a bright yellow bill. Note that the female is similar but very dark brown, with less of a yellow bill (see 87).

The starling, which is rather smaller, usually seems all black but is, in fact, a very dark brown. In bright light a greenish/purplish sheen may be noticed, especially in the breeding season, or a faint whitish speckle in winter, when it loses its yellow bill. Starlings are highly gregarious: huge flocks may be seen, often in towns and cities. They are unafraid of mankind and are usually found near human habitations.

Blackbird
male

Starling

winter

summer

What other colour did you notice?

(from 90)

Choose whichever colour was alone or mainly noticeable besides black.

Grey 45 White 93 Brown 94
Green 95

LESSER SPOTTED WOODPECKER m-f
GREAT SPOTTED WOODPECKER m-f
RING OUZEL m

R 14.5cm EW
R 23cm EWs
S 24cm EWSi

(from 92)

The two woodpeckers are rather similar, but are at once told apart by their size. The lesser spotted is no bigger than a chaffinch, while the great spotted is almost the size of a blackbird. The females of both species are entirely black and white. The males have some deep red plumage, the lesser spotted on the crown, the great spotted on the nape and under the tail.

There is no danger of confusion between the woodpeckers and the male ring ouzel. The former are

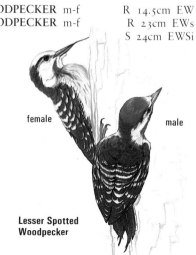

female

male

Lesser Spotted Woodpecker

Great Spotted Woodpecker

male

female

almost always seen on the trunks of trees or flying through woodland, while the ouzel, a summer visitor, is a bird of the open country, especially mountain and moorland. The male ring ouzel is like a male blackbird, but he has a conspicuous white crescent on his breast. Note that the female, though otherwise brown, also has a white crescent, but it is less noticeable (see 87).

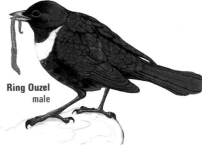

Ring Ouzel
male

94	**REED BUNTING** ms	R 15cm EWSI
(from 92)	**WHEATEAR** f	S 14.5cm EWSI
	QUAIL m	S 18cm Ewsi

Reed Bunting
male
(summer)

Wheatear
female

Quail
male

You should have no difficulty in distinguishing these three species. The male reed bunting is unmistakable in summer with his wholly black head, white collar and 'moustache', boldly marked back and wings, whitish breast and underparts. He is almost always found in reed beds, except in winter when he may appear on farmland. At that time of year, his head turns dark brown and he closely resembles the female (see 84).

The female wheatear often gives the impression of being wholly brown and white because the

black/white T-shaped pattern on her tail is easy to miss. Found exclusively in open country, she has a noticeable white rump and less prominent white eye-stripe. The male is more conspicuous (see 99). A summer visitor, as is the quail.

Quail are plump and rounded. They like quite long grass or standing corn, from which they are reluctant to emerge. When forced to break cover, they fly low with rapid wing-beats. The male has a black patch on his throat which is absent in the female (see 81), and a more strongly marked stripey head.

95 STARLING mfs-mfw R 21.5cm EWSI

(from 92)

The starling is rather smaller than a blackbird and usually seems all black, but in bright light a greenish/purplish sheen may be noticed, especially in the breeding season, when its bill is noticeably yellow.

Starlings are highly gregarious and may be seen in huge flocks, especially in towns and cities. Unafraid of man and usually found near human habitations.

96 Did it have a long tail?

(from 72)
Answer 'Yes' if the tail made up almost half the total length.

Yes 97 No 98

97 PIED WAGTAIL m-f s-w R 18cm EWSI
GREY WAGTAIL ms-mw-f R 18cm EWSI

(from 38, 96 and 189)

These two wagtails cannot possibly be confused. The pied wagtail, which is much the more common, is always grey and white, with areas of black that vary according to age, sex and season.

It is the yellow breast of the grey wagtail that always attracts attention. The head, back and tail are grey. In summer, the male has a

black bib; in winter this turns whitish and the sexes are almost identical.

Both species spend much time on the ground and are fond of walking. They do indeed wag their tails. The grey wagtail is usually found near water, whereas the pied wagtail, though not averse to water, may be seen in most habitats, often near human habitations. The flight of both is undulating.

The yellow wagtail is much scarcer. It also has a yellow breast, but no grey back (see 191).

98 Was it noticeably smaller than a blackbird?

(from 96)

Answer 'Yes' if it was about the size of a chaffinch. Answer 'No' if it was blackbird-size or larger.

Yes 99 No 100

99

DUNNOCK mf   R 14.5cm EWSI
BULLFINCH m-f   R 15cm EWSI
WHEATEAR m   S 14.5cm EWSI

(from 98)

Dunnock

male

female

Bullfinch

Wheatear
male

The dunnock, otherwise known (wrongly) as the hedge sparrow, is the only bird of the region with a grey head and breast. Note the slender bill, which is quite unlike the heavy bills of the sparrows. Found almost everywhere if some cover is available, the dunnock is relatively dowdy and cannot therefore be confused with the two other gaudy species.

The bullfinches and the male wheatear are very striking birds and easily distinguished. The wheatear is mainly a bird of the heathland and mountain, while the bullfinches prefer orchards, gardens, shrubbery and hedgerows.

The male bullfinch is extremely handsome, with his bright red breast, grey back and crown, black wingtips and tail. The female is a toned-down version of the male – pinkish brown where he is red, dark brown where he is grey. Despite their bright colours, the white rump of both sexes is often the most noticeable feature, if you see the bird only briefly, flying away into hedgerow or undergrowth.

The male wheatear, a summer visitor, also has a white rump, as does the brownish female (see 94). He is very conspicuous with his steel-grey crown and back, black wings and tail, and a black patch through and behind his eye. Exclusively a bird of open country, he is usually found on moorland and heather, though also on grassy uplands and sand dunes.

(from 98 and 135)

FIELDFARE mf
MISTLE THRUSH mf
PARTRIDGE m-f

W 25cm EWSI
R 27cm EWSI
R 30cm EWSi

Fieldfare

Mistle Thrush

male   female

Partridge

The fieldfare and mistle thrush are clearly members of the thrush family, and cannot be confused with the partridge, which is a game bird.

The fieldfare's grey head and rump are quite noticeable, but the greyness in the crown and back of the mistle thrush might well be missed. The two species are otherwise told apart firstly because the mistle thrush, which is larger, has a more boldly spotted breast; secondly because the fieldfare, a winter visitor, is almost always seen in flocks, while mistle thrushes are nearly always either solitary or in pairs. Both species are most at home in open, grassy country. The rattling flight-call of the mistle thrush is much more distinctive than the 'chak ... chak ... chak' of the fieldfare.

The partridge is quite different: brown and white with a conspicuous grey breast and orange-brown face and neck. The male has a chestnut horseshoe on his lower breast, which is normally absent, or almost absent, in the female. Partridge are usually in coveys, not easily flushed from their preferred cover of grass or corn. When disturbed, they fly noisily with rapid wing-beats.

(from 72)
Choose carefully from these four options the one that is most appropriate.

Breast only 102
Breast and wings 103
Under wings 104
Predominantly red 105

102

BULLFINCH m-f

R 15cm EWSI

(from 101)

The male bullfinch is extremely handsome: bright red breast, grey back and crown, black wingtips and tail. The female is a toned-down version of the male – pinkish brown where he is red, dark brown where he is grey.

Despite these bright colours, the white rump of both sexes is often the most noticeable feature, if the bird is seen only briefly as it flies away from you.

Bullfinches are most commonly seen in orchards, gardens, shrubbery and hedgerows. They are not at home in open country.

male

female

Bullfinch

103

BRAMBLING ms-mw-f

W 14.5cm EWSi

(from 101)

The male brambling in summer has an unmistakable black head and back but, as a winter visitor, he is seldom seen here in this finery. In winter, the black areas turn brown and he greatly resembles the female. In both sexes, the redness of the breast extends to the shoulders; and both have white rumps. Usually seen in parks, fields and gardens, often in flocks with other finches.

female

male (summer)

male (winter)

Brambling

104 · REDWING mf

(from 101)

The redwing is one of the two
thrushes – the other is the fieldfare
(see 100) – that arrive in flocks to
spend the winter with us. It can be
distinguished from all other thrushes
by its red flanks and underwing, its
prominent light eye-stripe and its
relatively small size. Usually seen in
open fields or in trees, sometimes in
company with fieldfares.

Redwing

105 · CROSSBILL m

R 16.5cm ewSi

(from 101)

The male crossbill is at once
distinguished by his bright red
colouring: he is by far the reddest-
looking bird of the region. The wings
and tail are darker. Usually seen in
conifers, often high up in the trees
and frequently in small flocks. The
crossed bill is not very noticeable.

Note that the female is green (see
108). If you saw red birds and green
birds in company, they are certain to
have been crossbills.

Crossbill

106 · Did it have a very long tail?

(from 72)
Answer 'Yes' if the tail made up
almost half the total length of the
bird.

Yes 191   No 107

| 107 |

YELLOWHAMMER m-f

R 16.5cm EWSI

(from 106)

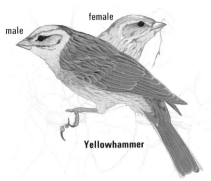

female

male

The yellowhammer is a bird of the fields and hedgerows, of woodland margins and clearings. It is the only species that gives the general appearance of being wholly brown and yellow. The male has a bright yellow head boldly marked with brown, and a yellow/brown breast and underparts. The female is a toned-down version of the male.

Yellowhammer

| 108 |

CROSSBILL f

R 16.5cm ewsi

(from 72)

The female crossbill is very green in general appearance, with darker wings. She is usually found in conifers, often high up in the trees and in small flocks. Her crossed bill is not very noticeable.

Note that the male is red (see 105). If you saw green birds and red birds in company, they are sure to have been crossbills.

Crossbill
female

| 109 |

What size was it?

(from 71)

You decided it was bigger than a blackbird (25cm). Now you have to decide if it was bigger than a rook (46cm). Birds close to rook-size will be found whichever answer is chosen.

Other common birds that are close to rook-size are the pigeon (41cm), the magpie (46cm), and the crow (47cm).

Rook-size or smaller 110

Bigger than a rook 150

| 110 |

Was it a jay?

(from 109)

Let us first eliminate the gaudy, noisy jay, which fits into no convenient category. Remove any doubts by glancing at 111.

Yes 111 No 112

(from 110)

The jay's plumage is generally pinkish brown. Its most reliable field marks are its white rump and wing-bars, very noticeable as it flies away from you. It has a black tail, black wing-tips and 'moustache'. These are much less easy to miss than its rather inconspicuous crest and its blue-black wing feathers.

The jay's flight is weak and undulating. It is usually its ugly call that first attracts attention – a loud squawk or screech. Generally seen in parks and gardens, often close to houses, but also in woodland or more open country with trees.

Jay

112   Was it a member of the dove family?

(from 110)

The familiar woodpigeon is a member of the dove family; other members bear a strong family resemblance to it, though they are always smaller and sometimes quite differently coloured. Doves are heavy and plumpish, with pointed wings and fast flight. All have their own versions of the woodpigeon's cooing 'song'.

Yes 113   No 116

Dove

Woodpigeon

113   What colour was it?

(from 112)

All truly wild members of the dove family fall easily into one or other of the categories below.

In many towns and cities, you will often see large congregations of half-tame pigeons, which may be any possible combination of blue-grey, purple, black, cinnamon-red, brown and white. These are known as feral pigeons; they are the descendants of domestic doves that escaped from captivity and interbred, often with rock doves (see 289) which are their own original ancestors.

Feral pigeons are not usually counted as a species of their own.

Mainly blue-grey/purple 114
Mainly brown/brownish 115

(from 113)

114 WOODPIGEON mf   R 41cm EWSI
STOCK DOVE mf   R 33cm EWsi

Woodpigeon

Stock Dove

The woodpigeon, which is much the more common, is distinguished by its greater size and by its noticeable white neck patches and wing-bars. The stock dove has no white plumage, is more compact, and flies more directly with faster wing-beats.

Note that the rock dove is not included here, but among the water birds (see 289), because it is virtually never seen in a truly wild state except on the coast. Birds identical to rock doves may occur among flocks of feral pigeons (see 113). They are very like stock doves but have white rumps.

115 COLLARED DOVE mf   R 32cm EWSI
TURTLE DOVE mf   S 27cm Ewsi

(from 113)

The collared dove is much the commoner. It often occurs in flocks, especially near human habitations where there is a plentiful supply of grain and it becomes semi-domesticated. The turtle dove, which is a summer visitor, prefers parks and gardens, or open country with scattered trees. It is noticeably darker than the collared dove, which is sand-coloured.

Otherwise these species are told apart by their neck markings and their voices. The collared dove has a black half-collar edged with white, and always coos three times, with emphasis on the second note. The turtle dove boasts strange white neck patches with a pattern of black stripes, and its soothing voice is more of a purr than a coo.

Collared Dove

Turtle Dove

116

(from 112)

Was it a bird of prey (other than an owl)?

Birds of Prey

There are six to choose from: three falcons, two harriers and a hawk. If at rest, they can be told by their short, curved beaks and powerful claws. But they are more often seen in flight, when their long tails and short necks provide a typical and unmistakable outline.

Yes 117   No 123

117

(from 116)

What colour was it?

You should have no trouble in deciding which of these colour combinations is most appropriate.

Brown/white only 118
Brown and blue-grey 121
Mainly grey 122

118

(from 117)

What size was it?

This question needs no elaboration.

Rook-size (46cm) 119
Definitely smaller than a rook 120

119

(from 118)

HEN HARRIER f   R 51cm eWSI
MONTAGU'S HARRIER f   S 46cm ewi

These two females are extremely hard to tell apart. Both of them are uncommon, especially Montagu's harrier, which is a summer visitor. She is slightly smaller and has a less conspicuous white rump. Otherwise the two species can best be distinguished by reference to the much smaller males, if these

happened to be in their company – though the males, which are predominantly light grey, resemble each other too (see 122).

The usual habitat of both species is the same: open country, moorland, swamps and sometimes fields.

For the even scarcer marsh harrier, see the supplementary list.

Hen Harrier
female

Montagu's Harrier
female

KESTREL f   R 34cm EWSI
MERLIN f   R 33cm eWSi
SPARROWHAWK f   R 38cm EWSI

The female kestrel's back and tail are reddish brown, barred with dark brown. The female merlin has a plain brown back and her tail is barred with white. The female sparrowhawk is distinguished by her barred breast and underparts.

For the main differences between these three species, irrespective of sex, see 121. Note that two of the three females are larger than their males.

121

(from 117)

KESTREL m   R 34cm EWSI
MERLIN m   R 27cm eWSi
SPARROWHAWK m   R 28cm EWSI

The male merlin may be distinguished from the two others by his small size – little bigger than a blackbird.

He and the male kestrel have blue-grey heads and tails. The male merlin has a wholly grey back.

The male sparrowhawk has much the same grey areas as the merlin but is distinguished by his barred breast and underparts.

Note that two of the three males are smaller than their females.

If it was hovering, it must have

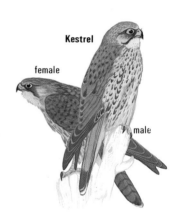

Kestrel
female
male

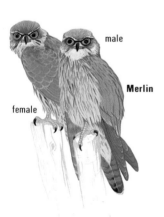

male
Merlin
female

female
male
Sparrowhawk

been a kestrel, much the commonest of the three.

The kestrel and merlin are falcons, which always have long pointed wings. The wings of hawks are shorter and blunter.

The two falcons are most easily distinguished by their habitats. The merlin, which is a very fast flyer, belongs to moorland and other open, treeless country, while the kestrel prefers farmland, cliffs, and fields with scattered trees.

Sparrowhawks are often recognized by their distinctive method of hunting. They fly near ground level along a hedgerow, then swiftly swoop up over it and down on the other side, to pounce on any prey there.

They like wooded country but appear in towns and villages.

122
(from 117)

PEREGRINE m	R	38cm ewsi
PEREGRINE f	R	48cm ewsi
HEN HARRIER m	R	43cm eWSI
MONTAGU'S HARRIER m	S	41cm ewi

The peregrine is a falcon and is told from the two harriers by its long, pointed wings, which are always a falcon's hallmark, and by its fast, dashing flight, sometimes aerobatic, or plunging earthwards, in typical 'anchor'-shape, after prey. The sexes are almost identical except for the considerable size difference.

The flight of the harriers has none of the peregrine's virtuosity. Both are light grey with black wing-tips. The only real differences between them are that Montagu's harrier has a black bar on the upper wing, faintly streaked brown underparts (not white) and no white rump. The brownish females are larger (see 119).

Both harriers favour very similar habitats – open country, moorland, swamps, sometimes open fields. Montagu's harrier is a summer visitor. The peregrines have the same preferences, but are more often associated with woodland or rough ground with scattered trees, or with estuaries and the coast, especially where there are cliffs.

For the scarcer marsh harrier, see the supplementary list.

Peregrine

Hen Harrier

male

male

Montagu's Harrier

(from 116)

123 · What was its main colour?

Ignore any secondary colour and
choose which of these was
predominant.

Brown 124 Black 138 White 145
Grey 148 Green 149

124 · What other colour did you notice?

(from 123)

Choose which other colour, if any,
you noticed along with brown.

Brown/white only 125
Grey 135 Black 137

125 · Was it a member of the thrush family?

(from 124)

The thrush and blackbird are well-
known to almost everyone. All other
members of the family bear a strong
likeness to them, and are easily
recognizable: they are much the same
size and shape, square-tailed, thin-
billed, and usually fine singers.

Yes 87 No 126

Thrushes

126 · Was it a member of the owl family?

(from 125)

Owls are almost always instantly
recognized as such, from their large
heads, large eyes, flattened faces,
short hooked beaks and powerful
claws. They cannot move their eyes
independently of their heads, so must
turn their whole head to look
around. Owls fly absolutely silently,
usually at dusk or at night.

Yes 127 No 129

Owls

127 · What size was it?

(from 126)

This question needs no elaboration.

Much the size of a blackbird 74
Much bigger than a blackbird 128

BARN OWL mf	R	34cm	EWsI
LONG-EARED OWL mf	R	36cm	ewSI
SHORT-EARED OWL mf	R	38cm	ewSI
TAWNY OWL mf	R	38cm	EWS

Barn Owl

Long-eared Owl

Short-eared Owl

Tawny Owl

The barn owl is easily told from the others because it is so lightly coloured. When, as is most usual, it is seen at dusk, or caught in the headlights of a car, it often seems all white. Its heart-shaped face also identifies it. Usually associated with old buildings, especially churches and barns. Its call is a blood-tingling shriek.

The long-eared owl is distinguished, as might be expected, by its very long ear tufts – it is the only British species in which they are clearly visible. More slender than the other owls, with a more elongated face, it may be seen in daytime sleeping in a tree, or at dusk hunting over open fields. Often frequents conifers. Its cry, which is seldom heard, is a low, plaintive hoot.

The short-eared owl is usually silent. It is the only owl that often hunts in daylight, and can best be distinguished from the tawny owl by its habitat. It likes very open country, marsh, moorland and mountain, while the tawny owl prefers woodland, parks and gardens, often near houses, and is even seen (or heard) in cities.

The tawny owl is the commonest of all – except in Ireland, where it is absent. It utters a very characteristic triple hoot: 'hoo ... hoo ... hoo-oo'. It roosts by day, usually in a deciduous tree, and is the most likely owl to be seen being mobbed by small birds that have spotted it.

For the much rarer snowy owl, which is mainly white, see the supplementary list.

(from 86 and 126)

Choose which of these habitats is most appropriate. 'Wetland' means any kind of very moist or swampy country.

Open fields (including corn) 130
Wetland 131 Woodland 132
Mountain and moor 133

130

(from 129)

PARTRIDGE m-f	R 30cm EWSi
GOLDEN PLOVER mfw	R 28cm EWSI
CORNCRAKE mf	S 27cm ewsi

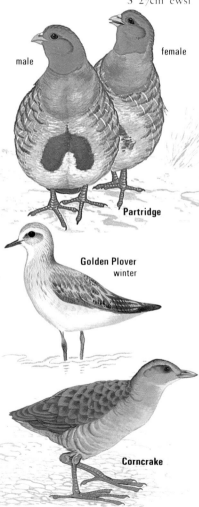

male

female

Partridge

Golden Plover
winter

Corncrake

These three species are quite easily told apart. The partridge, which is a game bird, is brown and white with a conspicuous grey breast and an orange-brown face and neck. The male has a chestnut horseshoe on his lower breast, which is normally absent, or almost absent, in the female. Partridge are usually found in coveys and are not easily flushed from their preferred cover of grass or corn. When disturbed, they fly noisily with rapid wing-beats.

In winter, the golden plover is brown with a whitish breast and underparts. At this time, it leaves the moor and mountain for dry, open fields or estuaries, where it is usually seen in flocks. In summer, it is much more distinctive (see 137).

I have written of other birds that they are more often heard than seen, but the corncrake – a summer visitor – is practically *never* seen, though its very loud, rasping, monotonous 'song' – '*crex . . . crex . . . crex*' – may fill the air unendingly, even at night. But if you try to flush it from the middle of an uncut meadow, where it almost always sings, you will seldom be successful. If you are, it will fly briefly, legs dangling, to another part of the meadow, and defiantly start singing again. It is undistinguished in appearance; rare in Britain and becoming scarce in Ireland.

131	**SNIPE** mf	R 27cm EWSI
	WOODCOCK mf	R 34cm EWSI
(from 129)	**REDSHANK** mf	R 28cm EwSi
	GREENSHANK mf	R 30cm ewSi

All four species have long bills, the snipe's being the longest, then the woodcock's. These two species have a strong family likeness, but the woodcock is more substantial and noticeably larger. It is more at home in woodland, but in mild weather may be found in open, wet country, where its flight when disturbed is much straighter than when it zigzags through the trees in its more usual habitat, and certainly straighter than the snipe's. It is further distinguished by its relatively blunt wings. Both species have boldly patterned heads.

For a comparison between the snipe and the similar but noticeably smaller jack snipe, see 76.

The snipe and woodcock are silent, except on the latter's 'roding flight' (see 132). The redshank and greenshank, when flying, usually utter a characteristic three-note whistle – '*peep . . . peep . . . peep*'; the latter's is the more musical. Both species have very conspicuous white rumps, and the redshank is distinguished in flight by an equally noticeable broad white band along the trailing edge of its wings. The redshank is a reddish brown, while the greenshank is lighter and greyer.

If seen at rest, the redshank is at once distinguished by its long, bright red legs. It also has a red bill, tipped with black. The greenshank's legs are equally long and are brownish, with only a hint of green. Its grey bill curves slightly upwards.

Snipe

Woodcock

Redshank

Greenshank

132	**WOODCOCK** mf	R 34cm EWSI
	NIGHTJAR m-f	R 27cm EWsi

(from 129)

The woodcock, which has a very long bill, is perhaps most often seen when on its so-called 'roding flight' in the breeding season. At this time, it flies quite low over the trees, with no hint of its usual zigzag, uttering every few seconds a most curious 'song' – two unmusical notes, followed by a croak. Otherwise it is most usually seen when flushed in woodland, flying off with a whirr of wings, dodging between the trees.

The nightjar is virtually never seen in broad daylight. Not long after sunset, it begins its strange churring 'song', which is what usually draws attention to it. A little while later it may take to the air, in silent flight as it searches for insects, looking rather like a hawk. The sexes are almost identical.

Woodcock

male

female

Nightjar

133   Did it have very long legs and bill?

(from 129)

Answer 'Yes' if it was a plain brown bird with long legs and a very long, down-turned bill. Answer 'No' if it was a game bird with legs and bill of normal length.

Yes 214   No 134

134 | **RED GROUSE** m-f | R 40cm EwSi |
| | **PTARMIGAN** fs | R 35cm S |

(from 133)

Both species are game birds, with short bills, heavy bodies and short, rounded wings. When flushed, they take to the air noisily with rapid wing-beats. They are easily told apart because red grouse in all seasons have fairly uniform all-brown plumage, while ptarmigan – even in summer – have extensive white areas on their wings and underparts. As autumn approaches, they become progressively whiter, till they are almost all white in winter (see 147).

Red grouse, which are often in coveys, are practically always found in heathery country, usually on mountain foothills or at least on high ground. Ptarmigan are confined to the Scottish highlands, almost always above the tree line. In summer they are usually in pairs, but often form flocks in winter.

The cock and hen ptarmigan are similar, but the male in summer is more greyish brown (see 136), the female more reddish brown. The red mark above the eye, known as the wattle, is more conspicuous in the male. In the red grouse, too, the sexes are very similar but again the male's wattle is more conspicuous; and the smaller hen is lighter in colour and more boldly barred. Note that the female black grouse is similar, but greyer (see 136).

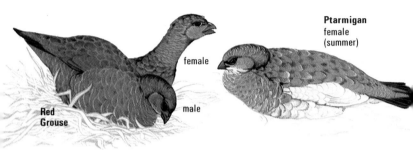

Ptarmigan
female
(summer)

female

male

Red
Grouse

135 Was it a member of the thrush family?

(from 124)
The thrush and blackbird are well known to almost everyone. All other members bear a strong family likeness to them, easily recognizable: they are much the same size and shape, square-tailed and thin-billed.

Yes 100   No 136

Thrushes

136

(from 135)

PARTRIDGE m-f
BLACK GROUSE f
PTARMIGAN ms

R 30cm EWSi
R 41cm ewS
R 35cm S

These three game birds are readily distinguished – apart from their size difference – by their habitats. The partridge belongs to farmland, especially where some cover is available. The black grouse is a bird of the uplands, preferring rough fields and moorland, or birchwood in winter. You will find the ptarmigan only in the Scottish highlands, almost always above the tree-line.

The partridge in any case looks quite different from the others. It is brown and white with a conspicuous grey breast and orange-brown face and neck. The male has a chestnut horseshoe on his lower breast, which is normally absent, or almost absent, in the female. Partridges are usually in coveys, not easily flushed from

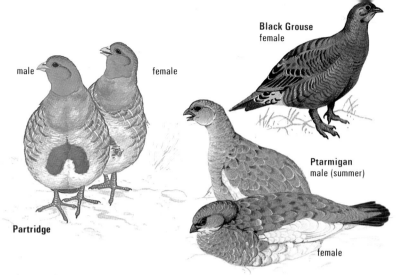

male female

Black Grouse
female

Ptarmigan
male (summer)

female

Partridge

their preferred cover of grass or corn. When disturbed, they fly noisily with rapid wing-beats.

The female black grouse, known as the greyhen, is rather like the red grouse (see 134) but is grey-brown with striking barred plumage. The male ptarmigan in summer is at once distinguished from her by the noticeable white plumage on his wings and underparts. The female

ptarmigan in summer has similar white areas, but is more of a reddish brown while the male is greyish brown. (The white plumage of both sexes becomes more extensive as autumn approaches, till they are almost all-white in winter; see 147.)

Note that the male black grouse, known as the blackcock, is much more distinctive, being almost all black and considerably bigger (see 163).

| 137 |

GOLDEN PLOVER mfs

R 28cm EWSI

(from 124)

The golden plover is very distinctive in summer, with its contrasting black cheeks, throat and underparts, edged with white; and it then belongs to the mountain and the moorland. During the winter, it becomes a rather insignificant, plain brown bird (see 130), leaving its summer habitat for dry open fields and estuaries. It is distinctly aerobatic and may be seen in flocks.

Note that the woodcock has a few black feathers, but these are so

Golden Plover
summer

inconspicuous that it is considered as being wholly brown and white (see 131).

138 What other colour did you notice?

(from 123)

Choose which other colour, if any, you noticed along with black.

Black only 139   White 141
Grey 144

139 What size was it?

(from 138)
This question needs no elaboration.

Blackbird-size or smaller 91
Rook-size 140

140

CARRION CROW mf   R 47cm EWS
ROOK mf   R 46cm EWSI

(from 139)

The carrion crow and rook are not very easily told apart. The adult rook has a bald white patch at the base of its beak, but this is absent in young birds. In any case it is often not very noticeable and both species are otherwise all black and much the same size.

The main distinguishing feature is the crow's way of cawing. The same note is usually repeated three times: '*caah ... caah ... caah*'. This is quite different from the rook's more varied voice. Also rooks are more sociable: they nest together in rookeries and are often seen in flocks, while crows nest on their own and are usually single or in pairs.

Carrion Crow

Rook

141 What size was it?

(from 138)
This question needs no elaboration.

Nearer to blackbird-size 142
Nearer to rook-size 143

GREAT SPOTTED WOODPECKER m-f
RING OUZEL m
LAPWING mf

R 23cm EWs
S 24cm EWSi
R 30cm EWSI

These three totally different species find themselves grouped together as the only black and white land birds of this size.

The great spotted woodpecker is exclusively a bird of the woodlands, both broad-leaved and coniferous. Both sexes have barred plumage and a red patch under the tail, but only the male has a red nape. Usually seen on the trunks of trees or flying through a wood. The lesser spotted woodpecker is similar but smaller (see 93).

The ring ouzel, a summer visitor, is a bird of the open country, especially mountain and moorland. The male is like a male blackbird, but told from it – apart from its different habitat – by the conspicuous white crescent on the breast. Note that the female, which is otherwise brown, also has a white crescent but it is less noticeable (see 87).

The lapwing, also known as the peewit or green plover, has distinctive black and white plumage; in bright sunshine, the black upper-parts have a noticeable greenish sheen. It is crested. Usually seen in flocks, often on farmland, grassland and moors.

male

Great Spotted Woodpecker

female

Ring Ouzel

Lapwing

male

MAGPIE mf   R 46cm EWSI
OYSTERCATCHER mf   R 43cm EWSI

These two species are both conspicuously pied, but the very common magpie is at once distinguished by its extremely long tail (half its total length).

The oystercatcher is normally a bird of the seashore, but is included here because it occasionally breeds inland, especially in Scotland. It is easily recognized by its long red beak and long pinkish legs.

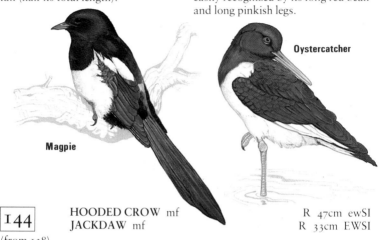

Oystercatcher

Magpie

HOODED CROW mf   R 47cm ewSI
JACKDAW mf   R 33cm EWSI

The hooded crow is much the larger and has far more extensive areas of grey plumage, which in the jackdaw are confined to the head and neck.

Jackdaws are often found near human habitations and frequently nest in chimneys, but 'hoodies' are shy of mankind. Apart from their grey plumage they are identical to carrion crows (see 140) – in habitat, voice and appearance – and sometimes interbreed with them.

Hooded Crow

Jackdaw

| 145 | Was it a member of the gull family?

(from 123)

Members of the gull family are most usually seen over or near water, but some species are found away from it and are therefore included among the land birds. Gulls are generally recognized by their all-white underparts and by their pearl grey backs and upper wings (which are, however, black or very dark grey in some larger species, see 153). Their wings are long and delicate and they have strong beaks and webbed feet.

Gulls

Yes 146 No 147

| 146 | **BLACK-HEADED GULL** mfs-mfw | R 37cm EWSI |
| | **COMMON GULL** mf | R 41cm EWSI |

(from 145)

These are the only two gulls included that are smaller than rook-size (for larger species, see 153). Both are misleadingly named because the common gull is not very common, and the black-headed gull has a chocolate brown head in summer, which turns white in winter – except for a small brown spot behind the eye.

The black-headed gull is much the most common of the species seen inland. In summer its dark brown head identifies it at once. And in all

seasons it can be distinguished by its smaller size, its more delicate flight, its narrower wings and its bright red beak and legs; those of the common gull are greenish yellow.

Black-headed Gull in winter

Black-headed Gull

summer

Common Gull

BARN OWL mf
PTARMIGAN mw-fw

R 34cm EWSI
R 35cm S

The barn owl is included here because, although it is brown and white, it very often gives the appearance of being an all-white bird when it is seen at dusk or is caught in a car's headlights. It is unmistakably an owl, flying on silent wings as it goes after its prey.

Nothing could be much more different than the ptarmigan, a game bird. In summer both sexes have extensive brown plumage which they lose progressively, till in winter they become pure white, apart from some black in the tail and, in the case of the male, a small black eye-stripe. They belong to the highlands of Scotland, where they are seldom seen under 600 metres.

Barn Owl

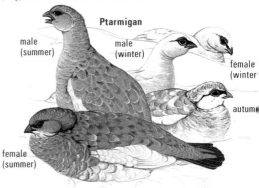

Ptarmigan

male
(summer)

male
(winter)

female
(winter)

autumn

female
(summer)

CUCKOO mf

S 33cm EWSI

The male cuckoo's voice, which is known universally, is almost always the first indication that a bird of this species is in the neighbourhood. If, shortly afterwards, you see a single hawk-like bird (but without the hawk's powerful beak and claws), usually flying rather low, it is almost sure to have been a cuckoo.

Cuckoos of both sexes are normally all-grey, except for their underparts which are white with brown bars. There is also a very rare all-brown form, heavily barred all over (females and young birds only).

Cuckoo

Cuckoos are summer visitors, seen in a very wide range of habitats.

If it gave the impression of being predominantly green, there is a chance it may have been a lapwing, also known as the peewit or green plover, which normally appears black and white, but whose black plumage, in bright sunshine, has a marked greenish sheen. The lapwing has a crest and is usually seen in marshy land or open fields.

However, it is much more likely to have been a green woodpecker, the

only bird of this size that is truly green in appearance – apart from the red crown in both sexes and the male's red 'moustache', which are not very noticeable. It in no way resembles the lapwing and is found in quite different country – almost always in woodland (usually broad-leaved), or in wooded parks and gardens.

Lapwing

female

male

Green Woodpecker

150   Did it have a long tail?

(from 109)

Answer 'Yes' if the tail made up almost half the bird's total length – or even more than half.

Yes |151| No |152|

These two species are quite different and have only their long tails in common.

The very comon magpie is entirely black and white; sometimes, in bright light, there is a greenish sheen

in the black plumage. It flies boldly out of cover and is often seen near houses in parks and gardens.

The pheasant, on the other hand, is a game bird, and usually stays in cover till flushed, when it flies off

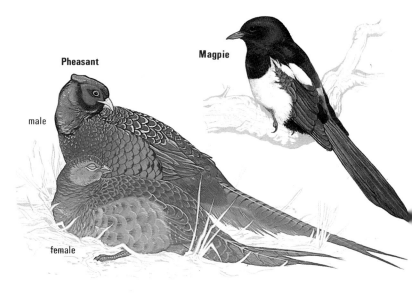

Pheasant

male

female

Magpie

with a whirr of wings. From time to time it may also be seen feeding at some distance in meadows or rough ground. Both sexes vary greatly in size from the average lengths given. The hen is a plain speckly brown. The cock – whose tail is even longer than the female's – is always unmistakable, with his blue/green head and red eye-patch.

Note that some cock pheasants have a white band round the throat, and others have yellower plumage. None of these counts as a separate species.

152   Was it a member of the gull family?

(from 150)

Members of the gull family are most commonly seen over or near water, but some species often occur away from it and are therefore included among the land birds. Gulls are usually recognized by their all-white underparts; their backs and upper wings may be pearl grey, dark grey or black, but they all have a generally white appearance. Their wings are long and pointed. They have strong beaks and webbed feet.

Gulls

Yes 153   No 154

Of the five gulls frequently seen inland, the black-headed – which is the commonest – is not included here because it is much smaller than a crow (see 146). The rather larger common gull, which is in fact the *least* common, is also smaller than a crow but is included for comparison because it is often confused with the herring gull.

The common gull and herring gull are both white below and pearly grey above, with white-flecked black wingtips. They are distinguished mainly by the difference in size, and also by the herring gull's stouter beak, which – unlike the common gull's – has a small red spot on it. Also the common gull has bright yellow legs, while the herring gull's are usually flesh-coloured.

The great black-backed and lesser black-backed gulls are easily distinguished from both the above because the whole of their backs and their upper wings are very dark grey (lesser black-backed) or black (great black-backed). They can also be told apart by the difference in size; and the latter has a much heavier bill.

Herring Gull

Common Gull

Lesser Black-backed Gull

Great Black-backed Gull

154
(from 152)

Was it a swan or a goose?

Swans and freshwater geese are primarily water birds, but are sometimes seen in fields some distance from lakes or rivers and are therefore included here. They are instantly told by their very long necks and great size. The swans, which are all pure white, are larger than the geese and have even longer necks. The freshwater geese are all mainly grey/brown, perhaps with a black neck.

Swan 225 Goose 226
Neither of these 155

Swans

Geese

155 What colour was it?

(from 154)
Carefully choose which of these four colour categories is appropriate.

Brown or brown/white 156

Black or black/white 161
Black and grey 164
Black and brown 165

156 Was it very long-billed?

(from 155)
Answer 'Yes' if it had an extremely long, down-turned bill and very long legs.

Yes 157 No 158

157 CURLEW mf R 56cm EWSI

(from 156)

It must have been a curlew. The similar whimbrel is very much smaller (see 214). It is usually the loud call – 'curlew, curlew' – that first draws attention to these very large birds. Immediately distinguished from all other waders by its size; its white rump is not very noticeable. The curlew belongs usually to coasts and estuaries, or to swampy land, but is also seen in dry fields.

Curlew

(from 156)

Birds of prey are recognized, when at rest, by their short curved beaks and powerful claws. But they are more often seen in flight, when their long tails and short necks provide a typical and unmistakable outline.

Birds of Prey

Yes 159   No 160

159	**BUZZARD** m	R	51cm eWSi
	BUZZARD f	R	56cm eWSi
(from 158)	**HEN HARRIER** f	R	51cm ewSI
	MONTAGU'S HARRIER f	S	46cm ewsi

The buzzard, which varies in colour from very light brown to almost black, is distinguished from the harriers by its very much heavier, eagle-like build. It has very well-feathered legs and a barred tail. Prefers woodland, except in winter when it may be found in open country. It sometimes hovers.

The two female harriers are not easy to tell apart. The rarer Montagu's harrier, which is a summer visitor, is slightly smaller and has a less conspicuous white rump. Otherwise the two species can best be distinguished by reference to the much smaller males, if these happened to be in their company, though the males, which are predominantly light grey, resemble each other too (see 122).

The usual habitat of both species is the same: open country, moorland, swamps and sometimes fields. For the even scarcer marsh harrier, see the supplementary list.

Buzzard

light form

dark form

Hen Harrier female

Montagu's Harrier female

The pheasant is very much the commoner and may be seen in fields, scrub and woodland almost anywhere. The capercaillie is wholly confined to the hills and mountains of Scotland, usually in coniferous woodland.

The hen pheasant is at once distinguished by her very long tail and far more slender build. She is speckled brown with paler underparts. The hen capercaillie, which is boldly barred, is similar to the female red grouse (see 134), but very much bigger and with a reddish patch on her breast. In both species, the males are very distinctive (see 151 and 165).

Capercaillie female

Pheasant female

---

161 Was it a member of the crow family?

(from 155)

Rooks and crows are well-known to almost everyone, and the three possible species, which are all wholly black, have a strong family likeness.

Yes 162 No 163

162	ROOK mf	R 46cm EWSI
	CARRION CROW mf	R 47cm EWS
(from 161)	RAVEN mf	R 64cm eWSi

The rook and carrion crow are not very easily told apart. The adult rook has a bald white patch at the base of its beak, but this is absent in young birds. In any case it is not very noticeable, and both species are otherwise all black and much the same size. The main distinguishing feature is the crow's way of cawing. The same note is usually repeated three times: '*caah . . . caah . . . caah*'. This is quite different from the rook's more varied voice.

Rooks are also more sociable: they nest together in rookeries and are often seen in flocks, while crows nest on their own and are usually single or in pairs.

The raven, which is much less common than either of the other two, is more a bird of the mountains, though it sometimes descends to the valleys and to remote wooded farmland. The most obvious difference is its far greater size, but this is less noticeable than might be

Rook

Carrion Crow

Raven

expected, especially at high altitude. Its most important distinguishing feature is then its wedge-shaped tail.

Ravens, which have very strong bills, are almost always single or in pairs. Their voice is very distinctive – much more of a croak than the others'.

| 163 | **BLACK GROUSE** m | R 53cm ewS |

(from 161)

The male black grouse is the only possibility left. He is mainly a bird of the mountain and moorland, but in winter his range extends to open woodland, especially birch. The male bird, known as the blackcock, usually gives the appearance of being all black with small white wing-bars, but in fact the upper wings are very dark brown. He cannot be confused with any other bird, except perhaps the male capercaillie (see 165), but the latter is much bigger and prefers coniferous woodland. Also the male

Black Grouse male

black grouse has a most unusual lyre-shaped tail.

The female, known as the greyhen, is brown and much smaller (see 136).

164

HOODED CROW mf

(from 155)

The hooded crow is the only large bird with extensive areas of black and grey plumage. The jackdaw is much smaller and only its head and neck are grey (see 144).

Note that hooded and carrion crows sometimes interbreed. The resultant hybrids have variable areas of grey plumage, but these never extend to the head.

Hooded Crow

165

BLACK GROUSE m
CAPERCAILLIE m

R 53cm ewS
R 86cm S

(from 155)

Both species are game birds and usually appear all black, but the upper wings in both cases are in fact dark brown; and the male black grouse, known as the blackcock, has rather inconspicuous white wing-bars.

The two species are told from each other because the blackcock is very

decidedly smaller and has a strange lyre-shaped tail. The capercaillie is confined to the coniferous woodlands of the Scottish highlands, and the black grouse to heath and woodland, especially birch in winter, in remote mountainous or hilly country. The brownish females are much smaller (see 136 and 160).

Black Grouse
male

Capercaillie
male

166   Where was it seen?

(from 1)

Note that the tidal mouths of rivers are treated as being salt.

On or near fresh water 167
On or near salt water including estuaries 232

167   What size was it?

(from 166)

In this part of the book, size is always reckoned by comparison with two very common species known by almost everyone: the blackbird (25cm) and the rook (46cm). Measurements given are from the tip of the bill to the tip of the tail.

Here you have to decide how the bird compared in size with a blackbird. Birds very close to blackbird-size will be reached whichever answer is chosen.

Other common birds that are close to blackbird-size are the song thrush (23cm) and the mistle thrush (28cm).

Blackbird-size or smaller 168
Bigger than a blackbird 192

168   What colour was it?

(from 167)

This question refers to the colour of the feathers; it ignores the legs and the bill.

The plumage of many birds is either brown or brown and white, and these are often among the hardest to identify. So, if a bird seems at first to be entirely brown or brown/white, always look carefully to see if any other colour is present.

Brown or brown/white *only* 169
Ignore brown and white. Choose which of the following was predominant.
Black 179   Blue 188   Grey 189
Red 190   Yellow 191

169   Was it a wader?

(from 168)

The six species of wader considered under this heading are all long-legged and rather long-billed. They are seen wading in shallow water or walking or standing near water or on marshy ground, or flying low over it. They usually have a rapid flight.

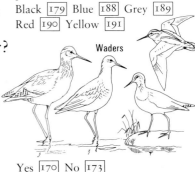
Waders

Yes 170   No 173

170   Did it have a white rump?

(from 169)

Answer 'Yes' if you noticed a conspicuous white rump as the bird flew away from you. If in doubt, consult both answers.

Yes 171   No 172

REDSHANK mf
GREEN SANDPIPER mf

R 28cm EwSi
W 23cm EWsi

(from 170)

The redshank, the larger and the
commoner of the two, has a
noticeable white bar along the
trailing edge of its wings. (So has the
common sandpiper, see 172.) This
combines with its white rump to
create an unmistakable pattern in
flight, when it often utters a
characteristic three-note whistle –
'*peep . . . peep . . . peep*'. Its bright red
legs and bill are often noticeable.

The green sandpiper is usually
seen when on passage in spring and
autumn, but a few birds stay the
winter. It is misleadingly named
because it isn't in the least bit green.
It is distinguished by its dark
upperparts, the dark underside of its
wings and its barred tail. It often has
a snipe-like flight.

Redshank

Green Sandpiper

SNIPE mf
JACK SNIPE mf
COMMON SANDPIPER mf
RUFF f

R 27cm EWSI
W 19cm EWSI
S 20cm EWSI
W 23cm Ewsi

(from 170)

Snipe

Jack Snipe

Common Sandpiper

Ruff
female

The two snipe, which are both
hunted by wildfowlers, are
practically never seen at rest, and will
only break cover as you approach.
Both species have long bills and
belong to marshy, boggy ground.
They are distinguished by their size
difference and also because, after
take off, the snipe has a very

characteristic zigzag flight and usually flies on out of sight. The jack snipe, which is a winter visitor, flies almost straight and not nearly so far (usually less than a hundred yards) before settling again in cover.

The common sandpiper, when inland, is most often seen on freshwater margins or flying low over a lake. A summer visitor, its most obvious field mark is the conspicuous white bar along the trailing edge of its upper wings. At rest it has a habit of bobbing its head and tail; in flight it often flicks its wings, with a momentary pause on each downstroke.

Ruffs are winter visitors. In winter the female, known as the reeve, closely resembles the male, except that the latter is considerably larger (see 217). Like the sandpiper, the ruff is most often seen on freshwater margins when inland, but hasn't the same fondness for flying low over water. In winter both sexes are undistinguished, but have heavily mottled backs and pale underparts. A white crescent is noticeable in flight on each side of the tail. The beak is rather short, and the legs are usually reddish.

---

173 | Was it a dipper?

(from 169)

If necessary, glance at 186 to decide if it was a dipper. If it wasn't, turn to 174.   Yes 186   No 174

---

174 | Was it noticeably larger than a chaffinch?

(from 173)

Of the five remaining possible species, two are about the size of blackbirds, while the others are chaffinch-size or smaller.   Yes 175   No 176

175

LITTLE GREBE mfw   R 27cm EwSI
WATER RAIL mf   R 28cm ewsI

(from 174)

These are the two smallest freshwater swimmers. In winter the little grebe, also known as the dabchick, is a rather inconspicuous brown/grey. Its summer plumage of chestnut and dark brown is more distinctive. The dabchick can be distinguished from the water rail because it is often seen swimming on open water. The rail hardly ever leaves the cover of reeds or rushes.

Even if it remains invisible, the water rail's presence can be detected in summer by its very extraordinary voice – a succession of extremely variable grunts and squeals, sounding something like a pig. It is much more often heard than seen. When it does put in an appearance, it can easily be told by its red bill, grey underparts and barred flanks.

For the rarer grebes, see the supplementary list.

winter

summer

Little Grebe

Water Rail

Was it like a brown and white swallow?

(from 174)
Answer 'Yes' if it looked like a brownish swallow (but without the long tail streamers), almost always

airborne on its long pointed wings, swooping low over the water.

Yes 177 No 178

| 177 |

SAND MARTIN mf

S 12cm EWSI

(from 176)

The sand martin is gregarious, nesting in colonies in holes in sandbanks (or sometimes gravel banks). In outline and in flight it is like a swallow, but with a short forked tail. It is brown with white underparts and a broad brown breast-band. Smaller than other swallow-like birds, it is a summer visitor.

Sand Martin

| 178 |

SEDGE WARBLER mf
REED WARBLER mf
REED BUNTING mw-f

(from 176)

S 13cm EWSI
S 12.5cm Ew
R 15cm EWSI

As their names imply, all three species are usually found in reeds or other vegetation by lakeside or riverside, though the reed bunting in winter may also appear on farmland. You can tell the warblers from the bunting because they have thin bills, while the bunting's is thick and heavier.

The two warblers, beside being rather secretive, are very inconspicuous and quite hard to distinguish, apart from their songs (see below). The sedge warbler is noticeably paler and has a fairly prominent white eye-stripe running from the beak over the eye to the neck. This is almost absent in the

Sedge Warbler

Reed Warbler

Reed Bunting

female

male
(winter)

reed warbler. The sedge warbler's upperparts are quite boldly streaked, while those of the reed warbler are almost plain brown.

Both species stay so well hidden that they are far more often heard than seen. Their voices are their most distinctive features: the reed warbler's is a rather monotonous '*chirruk, chirruk ... chirr, chirr*', the sedge warbler's a rapid intermingling of sweet and harsh notes.

Apart from their heavier bills, the reed buntings are distinguished from both warblers by their boldly patterned plumage. Note that, in summer, the male is at once recognized by his black head and throat with white collar and 'moustache' (see 180). The black areas turn dark brown in winter.

179

(from 168)

Was the black plumage confined to the head and throat?

This question needs no elaboration.   Yes 180   No 181

180

(from 179)

REED BUNTING ms   R 15cm EWSI

Reed Bunting
male
(summer)

The male reed bunting is unmistakable in summer with his wholly black head, white collar and 'moustache', boldly marked back and wings, pale underparts. Almost always found in reed beds, except in winter when he may appear on farmland. At that time of the year, his head becomes dark brown and he closely resembles the female (see 178).

181

Was it a member of the swallow family?

(from 179)

Members of the swallow family are all summer visitors with very long wings and forked tails. They are almost always seen in flight, except when at their nests or when they congregate on telephone wires in late summer.

Swallows

Yes 182 No 183

182

SWALLOW mf   S 19cm EWSI
HOUSE MARTIN mf   S 12.5cm EWSI

(from 181)

These two summer visitors are primarily land birds. They are included here because they often fly low over water to feed.

The red throat of the swallow is very seldom noticed. What really distinguishes it are its very long tail streamers, immediately seen as it passes overhead or wheels in the sunshine.

The house martin, which is substantially smaller, is equally easy to recognize, with its conspicuous white rump, hard to miss between

Swallow

House Martin

back and tail as it soars away from you. Both species have white underparts.

183

Did it have a long tail?

(from 181)
Answer 'Yes' if its tail was over one-third of its total length.

Yes 184 No 185

184

PIED WAGTAIL mf sw   R 18cm EWSI

(from 183)

It must have been a pied wagtail, which is very easy to recognize. Its plumage varies with sex, age and season, but is always a combination of black and/or slate grey with white. Its flight is weak and undulating; it is more often seen on the ground, perhaps in shallow water. Likes

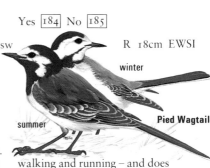

winter

summer

Pied Wagtail

walking and running – and does indeed constantly wag its tail when not airborne.

Was it a dipper?

(from 183)

If necessary, turn to 186 to decide if it
was a dipper; if it wasn't, turn to 187.   Yes |186| No |187|

| 186 |

DIPPER mf   R 18cm eWSI

(from 173
and 185)

The dipper is immediately
recognizable – a small, dark brown
bird, often looking black, with a
white breast. Always associated with
rivers, it is usually seen on a boulder
in midstream, constantly bobbing its
head. From there it may plunge into

Dipper

the river – it can swim strongly
underwater – or fly low over it.

| 187 |

LITTLE RINGED PLOVER mf   S 15cm E
RINGED PLOVER mf   R 19cm EWSI
DUNLIN mfs   R 18cm ewSi
GOLDEN PLOVER mfs   R 28cm EWSI

(from 185)

The black plumage of the two ringed
plovers is confined to the head and
neck. The two species are told apart
by the smaller size of the little ringed
plover, which alone is a summer
visitor, and the white bar on the
trailing edge of the ringed plover's
upper wings. The former has pink
legs while the latter's are red.

  The dunlin's black plumage is
confined to a large patch on its lower
breast, which is lost in winter (see
282). It is also distinguished from the
plovers by its longer, more pointed

bill, curving slightly downward. Like
the ringed plover, it is most often
seen on the seashore, but both may
visit inland marshes to nest.

  The golden plover in summer has

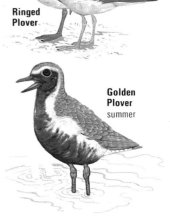

**Little
Ringed
Plover**

**Ringed
Plover**

**Golden
Plover**
summer

Dunlin
summer

much more extensive black plumage than any of the above (this is wholly lost in winter, see 284). Conspicuously edged with white, it extends from the head and neck all the way to the belly. Its crown and upperparts are a distinctive golden brown, mottled with black, and it is very noticeably larger than the other three species.

---

188   **KINGFISHER** mf   R 16.5cm Ewsi

(from 168)

Seeing a kingfisher – however often – remains one of the great joys of bird-watching, if not of life. The brilliant blue-green flash of its plumage as it streaks in direct flight at water level up or down a river with rapid wing-beats, or sits perched in a bush beside a river to fish, is never forgotten. Its brilliant plumage – note the chestnut underparts – combines with its large

Kingfisher

head and very heavy beak to make it wholly unmistakable.

---

189   ## Did it have a long tail?

(from 168)
Answer 'Yes' if its tail made up over one-third of its total length.

Yes 97 No 222

---

190   **LITTLE GREBE** mfs   R 27cm EwSI

(from 168)

The little grebe, also known as the dabchick, is seldom very conspicuous: it prefers lakes surrounded by reeds or rushes in which it may hide, but it is also quite often seen swimming in open water. In winter it is all brown and white (see 175); in summer its cheeks and neck become noticeably chestnut,

Little Grebe
summer

and it has a small white spot at the base of its bill.
    For the rarer grebes, see the supplementary list.

---

191   **GREY WAGTAIL** ms-mw-f   R 18cm EWSI
                YELLOW WAGTAIL m-f   S 16.5cm EWsi

(from 65, 106 and 168)

These two species are at once recognized by their long tails and bright yellow underparts. Both have pale eye-stripes. The grey wagtail, which is much the commoner, is distinguished by its slate-grey

upperparts and tail. Those of the yellow wagtail, which is a summer visitor, are brownish-green in the male, and yellowish-brown in the female. Its tail is slightly shorter.

The male grey wagtail in his breeding plumage has a noticeable black throat; this is white during the rest of the year when he becomes almost identical to the female.

Both species are often seen on the ground and they do indeed frequently wag their tails. Their flight is rather weak and undulating.

female

male (winter)

Grey Wagtail

male (summer)

Yellow Wagtail

female

male

192   Was it a member of the duck family?

(from 167)

Ducks appear in many different colours and sizes, but they all have more or less the same shape and general duck-like appearance. They have long necks (but not as long as geese), which are very noticeable when they fly, flattened beaks, short legs and webbed feet.

The colour of its speculum (plural specula) is sometimes important in identifying a duck. This is the name given to the brightly-coloured

Ducks

feathers along the trailing edge of its inner wing (see 202).

Yes 193   No 207

193   What size was it?

(from 192)

Of the fourteen freshwater species included here, three are noticeably smaller than average and five are noticeably larger than average. Note that the mallard – much the commonest of all – is one of the latter.

Below average for a duck   194
Above average for a duck   195
Average for a duck   198

TEAL m-f
GARGANEY m-f
SMEW m-f

R 35cm EWSI
S 38cm Ewi
W 41cm Es

The small size of the teal is so noticeable that the species can usually be identified at a great distance, as a flock flies in close formation with rapid wing-beats. If observed at rest (almost always swimming), the drake is highly distinctive, with a broad green eye-stripe running back through his chestnut head, and a bright green speculum. The female, which looks like a very small female mallard, is an inconspicuous brown, but she too has a green speculum.

Teal
female

male

The garganey is a summer visitor, more slender than the two others, and less often seen in flocks than the teal. The drake is quite easily distinguished, apart from his small size, by the white stripe running from just in front of the eye all the way back to the neck. The plain brown female is unremarkable, but in flight her blue-grey upper fore-wing may be noticed.

female   Garganey

male

Smews, which are winter visitors, are very much more distinctive. The drake, when swimming, gives the impression of being an almost all-white bird. In flight, his black wing-tips and wing-bars are visible, giving him a pied appearance. The female is the same but has grey plumage instead of black – and her red-brown head is quite noticeable.

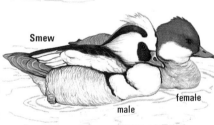

Smew

female

male

195

(from 193)

Was it a sawbill?

Sawbills are very large ducks, as big as the smallest geese. They are usually crested, and their long, thin beaks have down-turned tips. The males have green heads, the females reddish-brown heads.

Yes 196   No 197

RED-BREASTED MERGANSER m-f	R 58cm ewSl
GOOSANDER m-f	R 66cm ewS

The goosander drake has a hardly perceptible crest; the duck has a single crest. The male and female mergansers both have double crests, and the drake is further distinguished by his conspicuous reddish-brown breast. By contrast the male goosander has a white breast and underparts, very slightly tinged with pink.

Both drakes have a noticeably black-and-white appearance, especially in flight. The ducks are a less conspicuous grey. The female goosander has a sharp division between her brown head and her white neck and throat; the transition is much more gradual in the merganser.

The goosander is seen on inland waters throughout the year. The merganser is more of a sea bird but often visits lakes and reservoirs in the breeding season. Both species are very proficient divers.

female

Red-breasted Merganser

male

Goosander female

male

MALLARD m-f	R 58cm EWSI
SHELDUCK m-f	R 61cm EWSI
PINTAIL m	R 66cm ewsi
PINTAIL f	R 56cm ewsi

The drakes of these three large species are highly distinctive, and the female shelduck is very like the male.

The mallard is much the commonest and best-known of all ducks. The male bird has an irridescent head, which appears emerald green in some lights and peacock blue in others. There is a narrow white band between this

plumage and his chestnut breast. He has a bright blue speculum. The female has a similar blue speculum but is otherwise plain speckled brown.

The less common shelduck, more often found by the sea or on mud-flats, is quite unmistakable with its bright red bill and vividly contrasting green/white/chestnut plumage.

Mallard

Shelduck

Pintail

(Note that the green feathers look black, except in bright light.) The sexes are almost identical, apart from the knob at the base of the drake's bill.

The pintail is much scarcer than the two others, and also more slender. Both sexes have long tails, but the drake's is very much longer than the duck's. He is predominantly grey, with a brown head, but his

breast and neck are white. This white area continues upwards as a narrowing stripe to just behind the eye. The female is undistinguished apart from her fairly long tail. Pintails are mainly winter visitors but a few birds are here all year.

198 What colour was it?

(from 193)
Carefully choose which of these four colour categories is most appropriate.

Head green 199
Head reddish brown 200
Mainly black and white 201
Mainly brown 202

199

(from 198)

GOLDENEYE m
SHOVELER m

W 46cm ewSi
R 51cm EWsI

Goldeneye male

Shoveler male

The mallard drake also has a green head but has been eliminated because it is one of the larger ducks (see 197).

The goldeneye drake is mainly distinguished by the prominent white blob in the dark green plumage of its head, just in front of the eye. He has a white neck and underparts and is otherwise mainly black and white. Note that the female has a reddish brown head with no white blob (see 200). Goldeneye, which are winter visitors, can always be told in flight because their wings make a characteristic whistle.

The drake shoveler is rather like a mallard but, apart from being smaller, has a white breast, bright chestnut flanks and no white neckband at the base of his green head. At a distance, his very large, flattened bill is surprisingly inconspicuous. For the much plainer female, see 203.

200	WIGEON m	R 46cm EWSI
(from 198)	POCHARD m	R 46cm EWSI
	GOLDENEYE f	W 46cm ewSi
	SMEW f	W 41cm Es

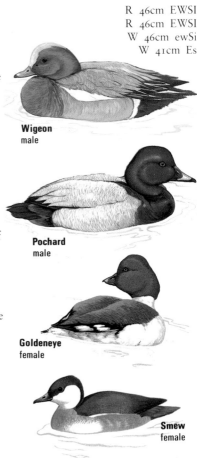

Wigeon
male

Pochard
male

Goldeneye
female

Smew
female

All four are winter visitors, but some wigeon and pochard stay all year.

The drake wigeon is easily distinguished by the yellow stripe running back from his bill to his crown. Otherwise he has an all-chestnut head; the rest of his body is grey and white with a darker tail.

The pochard drake has a plain, reddish-brown head. His black breast and tail are in strong contrast with his white flanks and belly. His upper wings are grey. The females of both species are mainly brown (see 203 and 206 respectively).

The head of the female goldeneye is chocolate brown. The rest of her body is light grey with white underparts. Goldeneye can always be told in flight because their wings make a characteristic whistle. The male's head is dark green, but sometimes looks black (see 199).

The dark brown head of the female smew does not extend below the beak line. The rest of the head is white, the rest of the body grey. For the very white-looking drake, see 201.

TUFTED DUCK m
GOLDENEYE m
SMEW m

R 43cm EWSI
W 46cm ewSi
W 41cm Es

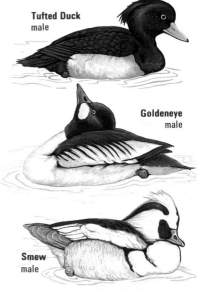

Tufted Duck
male

Goldeneye
male

Smew
male

The male tufted duck is much the most likely answer. He is all black except for the bold contrast of his white flanks and belly, and he has a rather droopy crest. The female, whose crest is less noticeable, is a more uniform sooty brown (see 205). Very fond of diving.

The two others are winter visitors. By virtue of his dark green head, the male goldeneye has already been considered (see 199), but the head may have seemed black to you, in which case he will have appeared to be all black and white. The white blob in front of the eye is noticeable. For the brown-headed female, see 200. Goldeneye can always be told in flight because their wings make a characteristic whistle.

The smew is somewhat smaller than both the others. Both sexes are very distinctive. The drake, when swimming, almost gives the impression of being an all-white bird.

In flight he shows his black wing-tips and wing-bars, which give him a pied appearance. For the greyer, red-headed female, see 200.

| 202 |

Did it have a blue or green speculum?

(from 198)
For an explanation of the word 'speculum', see 192.

Yes | 203 | No | 204 |

Speculum

| 203 |

(from 202)

MALLARD f
SHOVELER f
WIGEON f

R 58cm EWSI
R 51cm EWsI
R 46cm EWSI

These three females are predominantly brown, and not very easy to tell apart. The mallard, which has a blue speculum, is much commoner than the two others and noticeably bigger. The shoveler and wigeon show a green speculum. The former has a large, strangely flattened bill, which is however less noticeable than might be expected, and displays a light blue upper fore-wing.

The female wigeon is the smallest of these, and is distinguished only by her relatively small size, shorter beak and white belly. In most areas she is only seen in winter.

For the drakes of these three species, which are often in company and are all very distinctive, see 197, 199 and 200 respectively.

Mallard
female

Wigeon
female

Shoveler
female

204   Was it sooty brown?

(from 202)

One of these difficult females is very noticeably a dark sooty brown and has a small droopy crest, though this is not very conspicuous.

Yes 205   No 206

205   TUFTED DUCK f

(from 204)

R 43cm EWSI

Tufted Duck
female

The female tufted duck, with her sooty brown plumage, is quite different from any of the others. She is usually in company with the extremely distinctive black and white drake (see 201). The duck's crest is less conspicuous than the drake's. Very fond of diving.

206

POCHARD f
PINTAIL f
GADWALL m-f

(from 204)

R 46cm EWSI
W 56cm ewsi
R 51cm ewsi

The female pochard – much the commonest of the three – repeats in brown and grey the gaudier colours of the drake (see 200). She has a light ring round the eye and a light stripe running back from it. A resident, but in many areas is seen in winter only.

The female pintail hasn't such an excessively long tail as the male (see 197) but it is still quite long and pointed. Otherwise she has no real distinguishing marks. A winter visitor but some birds stay all year.

The male gadwall is the only drake that is predominantly brown – though it is rather a greyish-brown. His tail coverts are black. The drake and the less grey duck have the same distinctive colour scheme on their upper wings: a chestnut wing bar

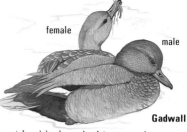

Pochard female

female

male

Gadwall

Pintail female

with a black and white speculum. This pattern is most clearly seen in flight but may also be visible at rest. Although it is a resident, many more birds are seen in winter.

 207

Was it a gull or a tern?

(from 192)

Gulls and terns are recognizable as such because they are mainly white and pearl grey. Though some species have black wing-tips and others have backs and upper wings that are wholly black or dark grey, they all have a generally white appearance.

Both families have long pointed wings, but the terns' are even longer and narrower than the gulls'. Terns are also distinguished by their tails, which are forked not square, their black crowns and their even more delicate flight.

Furthermore, gulls are surface feeders, while terns sometimes dive

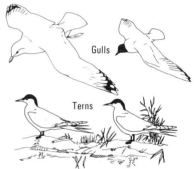

Gulls

Terns

into the water to seek small fish below the surface.

Gull 208 Tern 260
Neither of these 209

208

What colour were its back and upper wings?

(from 207)

This question needs no elaboration.

Black or dark grey 254
Mainly pearl grey 257

209

What size was it?

(from 207)

You have decided that it was bigger than a blackbird (25cm). Now you have to decide if it was bigger than a rook (46cm). Birds close to rook-size

will be found whichever answer is chosen.

Rook-size or smaller 210
Bigger than a rook 224

210   Was it a great crested grebe?

(from 209)

If necessary, glance at 211 to decide if
it was a great crested grebe. If it
wasn't, turn to 212.

Yes 211   No 212

211   GREAT CRESTED GREBE mfs-mfw   R 48cm Ewsl

(from 210)

These unusual birds are almost
always seen, either singly or in pairs,
well out towards the middle of a
wide expanse of water. They
practically never fly, but are very
expert divers and will evade pursuit
by prolonged underwater swimming,
surfacing only to take a quick breath.
In summer they are quite
unmistakable with their very
conspicuous ear-tufts and chestnut
'frill'. These disappear in winter,
when their white cheeks, neck and
breast become conspicuous. In all
seasons their pink bills are pointed
and quite long.

Great Crested Grebe

summer   winter

212   What colour was it?

(from 210)

This question refers to the colour of
the feathers; it ignores the legs and
bill.

    The plumage of many birds is
either brown or brown and white –
and these are often the hardest to
identify. So, if a bird seems at first to
be brown/white, always look

carefully to see if any other colour is
present.

Brown or brown/white only 213
Ignore brown and white – choose
which of the following
predominates.
Black 218   Grey 222   Green 223

213   What size was it?

(from 212)

Turn to 214 if it was nearly as big as
a rook (46cm). Turn to 215 if it was
definitely smaller than this.

Nearly rook-size 214
Not nearly rook-size 215

WHIMBREL mf   S 41cm ewsi

(from 133
and 213)

Whimbrels sometimes nest in the
Scottish islands and may occur
elsewhere in summer, but they are
mainly seen as passage migrants
passing through the British Isles on
their way between their breeding
grounds and their winter quarters in
spring and autumn. They are like
small curlews (see 231), with long
legs and long down-curved bills.
Apart from their appreciably smaller
size, they are distinguished from

Whimbrel

them by their boldly striped crowns
and faster wing-beats. Though
sometimes seen inland, they are more
often found on coastal mud-flats.

| 215 | Did it have a white rump?

(from 213)
Answer 'Yes' if it had a noticeable
white rump. If in doubt about this,
consult both answers.   Yes | 216 | No | 217 |

| 216 | **REDSHANK** mf   R 28cm EwSi
           GREENSHANK mf   R 30cm ewSi
(from 215) **GREEN SANDPIPER** mf   W 23cm EWsi

The redshank, which is generally the
commonest of these, has a broad
white bar along the trailing edge of
its upper wings which, combined
with its rump, produces a noticeable
white pattern in flight. (Note that the
smaller common sandpiper has a

Redshank

Greenshank

Green Sandpiper

similar white bar but no white rump, see 172.) The redshank is also recognized by its bright red legs and by its red bill tipped with black.

The redshank and greenshank both have a characteristic whistle – the same note, usually repeated three times. The greenshank is slightly larger, its upperparts greyer and its belly noticeably lighter. Despite its name, its legs are not very green, but rather pale with a tinge of olive.

Greenshanks are mainly summer visitors but a few birds stay for the winter.

The green sandpiper is most often seen on passage in spring and autumn, but again some birds stay the winter. It is misleadingly named because it isn't the least bit green. Distinguished by its dark upperparts, the dark underside of its wings and its barred tail. It zigzags in flight, like the snipe.

2 I 7	**SNIPE** mf
	RUFF mw
(from 2 I 5)	**RUFF** f

The snipe is practically never seen except when flushed from cover. It is then at once recognized by its dodging, zigzag flight, as it heads for safety across the moor or bogland, usually flying on till out of sight. It has a very long bill. For the much smaller jack snipe, see 172.

Ruffs are winter visitors. In winter, the male and female closely resemble each other, but the female, known as the reeve, is noticeably smaller. When inland, they are most often seen on freshwater margins. Both sexes are undistinguished in winter, but have heavily mottled backs and pale underparts. A white crescent is noticeable in flight on each side of the tail. Ruffs have short beaks and usually reddish legs.

R 27cm EWSI
W 29cm Ewsi
W 23cm Ewsi

Snipe

Ruff
male (winter)

female

2 I 8	What other colour (if any) did you notice?
(from 2 I 2)	

This question needs no elaboration.

All or almost all black 2 I 9
Markedly black and white 220
Black and brown 221

219

MOORHEN mf
COOT mf

R 33cm EWSI
R 38cm EWSI

(from 218)

These two very common species may
be seen almost everywhere on or
beside protected expanses of water,
especially ponds and rivers.

They are easy to tell apart. You
cannot fail to notice the pure white
'shield' of the coot, which rises from
the base of its white bill. The
moorhen has a similar if less
noticeable red shield, and a red bill
tipped with yellow. Moreover the
coot's plumage is all black, while the
moorhen (also known as the
waterhen) has a few white feathers in
its wings and under its tail.

Note also that the moorhen, when
swimming or walking, always bobs
its head backward and forward.

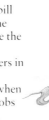

Moorhen

Coot

220

LAPWING mf
OYSTERCATCHER mf

R 30cm EWSI
R 43cm EWSI

(from 218)

Neither of these species is most
frequently seen near fresh water, but
the lapwing sometimes occurs in
marshy country and the
oystercatcher occasionally nests in
hilly river valleys, especially in
Scotland.

Both species are boldly pied, but
the lapwing (also known as the
peewit or green plover) is crested and
much smaller. In bright light its
plumage may have a definite greenish
tinge. Both species have rather long
pinkish legs, but the oystercatcher is
readily distinguished by its long,
bright red bill.

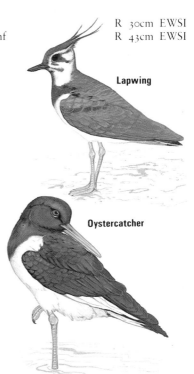

Lapwing

Oystercatcher

GOLDEN PLOVER mfs
GREEN SANDPIPER mf

R 28cm EWSI
W 23cm EWsi

The golden plover in summer is quite unmistakable. Its black plumage edged with white, which is completely lost in winter (see 284), extends from the head and neck all the way to the belly. Its crown and upperparts are a distinctive golden brown, mottled with black.

The green sandpiper is most often seen on passage in spring and autumn, but a few birds stay the winter. Much scarcer than the plover and with a much longer bill, it has no really black plumage, but its upper and lower wing-surfaces are very dark, in strong contrast with its white rump and barred tail. It is misleadingly named because it isn't the least bit green. It zigzags in flight, like a snipe.

Golden Plover summer

Green Sandpiper

WATER RAIL mf

R 28cm ewsI

The water rail is exceedingly elusive. It spends almost its whole life in reeds or undergrowth surrounding a lake or along a river, from which it can hardly be flushed. However, it occasionally takes a short flight – usually back to cover as you approach – with legs dangling in the water. You may then have noticed its red bill, grey underparts, heavily barred flanks and pure white below the tail.

In summer the water rail's presence is usually detected by its extraordinary voice: a succession of extremely variable grunts and

Water Rail

squeals, sounding something like a pig. It is far more often heard than seen.

223

LAPWING mf

R 30cm EWSI

Lapwing

(from 212)

The lapwing, also known as the peewit or green plover, has distinctive black and white plumage. In bright sunshine, the black upperparts have a noticeable greenish sheen. It is crested. Usually seen in flocks, often on farmland, grassland and moors.

224   Was it a swan or goose?

(from 209)

Swans and geese are instantly distinguished by their very long necks and great size. The swans, which are all pure white, are larger than the geese and have even longer necks. Geese are all either mainly brownish grey (perhaps with a black neck) – these are known as Grey Geese – or wholly black and white, which are known as Black Geese.

Swans

Geese

Swan 225 Goose 226
Neither of these 227

225

MUTE SWAN mf
WHOOPER SWAN mf
BEWICK'S SWAN mf

R 152cm EWSI
W 152cm ewSI
W 122cm ewSI

(from 154, 224 and 232)

The odds are that it was a mute swan, the only resident, which is common and well-known on lakes and rivers almost everywhere. It is distinguished from the others by its bright orange bill, which has a characteristic black knob at its base. It is indeed mute (apart from an occasional grunt). On fresh water it is usually seen singly or in pairs, especially in summer.

Mute Swan

The two winter visitors arrive in flocks in October or November. Far from mute, they broadcast a honking chorus like so many geese. They are also distinguished from the mute swan by their lemon yellow bills, tipped with black, and not knobbed.

The whoopers and Bewicks are quite hard to tell apart. The considerable difference in size is less noticeable than might be imagined. The only certain distinction is in their beaks: the yellow area is greater in the whooper and comes to more of a point. The Bewick's call is less strident and more musical than the whooper's.

Whooper Swan

Bewick's Swan

226

(from 154 and 224)

CANADA GOOSE mf   R 97cm Ewsi
GREYLAG GOOSE mf   W 81cm eSi
PINK-FOOTED GOOSE mf   W 68cm ES
WHITE-FRONTED GOOSE mf   W 71cm EWSI

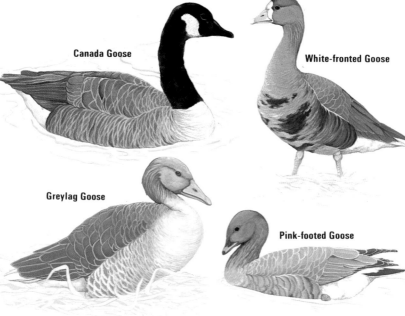

Canada Goose

White-fronted Goose

Greylag Goose

Pink-footed Goose

Of the six species of goose included in this book, two are associated with fresh water, two with salt water and estuaries (see 233) and two with either. All vary greatly in size from the average lengths given.

The Canada goose is the only resident, and the only Grey Goose to have a black neck and white cheeks and throat.

The three other freshwater species, which are winter visitors, are all Grey Geese and rather hard to tell apart. The greylag is the largest, the most heavily built and the greyest, though otherwise rather undistinguished apart from its pink legs and feet.

The pink-footed goose is smaller, has a darker head and neck, a shorter bill and rather more slender build. The white-fronted goose is more easily identified by the white at the base of its bill and the black marks on its belly. Also it has yellow legs and feet.

227 Did it look all black?

(from 224)

Answer 'Yes' if it appeared to be all black (apart from white cheeks and chin), even though it may in fact have been very dark blue/brown.

Yes 228   No 229

228 CORMORANT mf

(from 227)

R 90cm EWSI

The cormorant is the only large bird associated with fresh water (though more often with the sea) that appears all or mainly black, though it does have inconspicuous white patches on its cheeks and thighs. A skilful diver, it is usually seen on its own towards the centre of a lake, or flying over water. Its outline in flight, with its long neck held forward, is like a duck's, but its large size and black silhouette distinguish it at once.

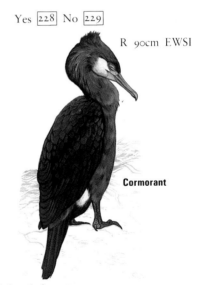

Cormorant

229 Did it have webbed feet?

(from 227)

If it was swimming, it certainly had webbed feet; and the only two possibles are almost invariably seen either swimming or diving.

Yes 230   No 231

These two members of the diver family are recognized by their characteristic streamlined shape, which also accounts for their remarkable diving ability. Except when at their nests, they spend almost all their lives either on or under the water.

The red-throated is the more common: it may be seen on freshwater lakes and reservoirs all year, though in summer it is almost wholly confined to Scotland. The black-throated is primarily a sea bird, and normally is seen inland only in the summer, when it most often nests on rocky islands in remote, secluded lakes.

The two species are told apart in summer by the colour of their backs:

the red-throated is grey-brown, the black-throated is barred black and white. They are also distinguished, though less easily, by the colour of their throats, which are indeed respectively reddish-brown and black, and the red-throated diver has a slightly upturned bill.

In winter they are almost identical apart from the slight difference in size. However, if it was seen on fresh water in winter, it is much more likely to have been the red-throated, which is slightly lighter coloured.

Red-throated Diver

winter

summer

summer

winter

Black-throated Diver

231

CURLEW mf   R 56cm EWSI
GREY HERON mf   R 90cm EWSI
OYSTERCATCHER mf   R 43cm EWSI

(from 229)

These three very different species can hardly be confused. The curlew is by far the largest of the waders, with very long legs and a long down-turned bill. For the similar but much smaller whimbrel, see 214.

The heron is even bigger, and is at once distinguished by its extremely

long neck and legs, and by its grey and white plumage with less noticeable black crest. The oystercatcher is conspicuously black and white, with a long red bill and long red legs.

Oystercatchers are primarily birds of the coast, and are included here

Grey Heron

Curlew

Oystercatcher

in shallow water, but they nest in colonies in the topmost branches of high trees.

only because they sometimes nest inland, usually not far from rivers or on moorland. Herons are most commonly seen singly, often fishing

Curlews may be seen almost anywhere on marshy ground or moorland, and also in dry fields. It is their loud call, 'cur*lew*, cur*lew*' that usually attracts attention.

232   Was it a swan or goose?

(from 166)

Swans and geese are instantly distinguished by their very long necks and great size. The swans, which are all pure white, are larger than the geese and have even longer necks. Geese are all either mainly brownish grey – these are known as Grey Geese – or wholly black and white, which are known as Black Geese.

Swan 225   Goose 233
Neither of these 234

Swans

Geese

GREYLAG GOOSE mf   W 81cm eSi
WHITE-FRONTED GOOSE mf   W 71cm EWSI
BARNACLE GOOSE mf   W 63cm sl
BRENT GOOSE mf   W 59cm ei

Greylag Goose

Of the six species of goose included, two are associated with the sea and estuaries, two with fresh water (see 226) and two with either.

These four are all winter visitors. They greylag and the white-fronted, both Grey Geese, are wholly grey-brown except that the latter, which is appreciably smaller, has a white band running round the base of its bill and some black marks on its belly. The greylag has noticeably pink legs and feet, while those of the white-fronted are yellow.

The barnacle and brent, on the other hand, are Black Geese. No larger than the very biggest of the ducks, they are easily told apart because the barnacle goose has a striking black/white head pattern and a pure white belly and flanks. Both have black legs.

There are two distinct subspecies of brent geese – dark-breasted and light-breasted. The former is much the commoner.

White-fronted Goose

Barnacle Goose

dark-bellied form

light-bellied form

Brent Goose

Was it a member of the duck family?

(from 232)

Ducks appear in many different colours and sizes, but all have more or less the same shape and general duck-like appearance. They have long necks (but not as long as geese), which are very noticeable when they fly, flattened beaks, short legs and webbed feet.

Ducks

The colour of its speculum (plural specula) is sometimes important in identifying a duck. This is the name of the brightly-coloured feathers along the trailing edge of its inner wing.

Yes 235   No 252

Did it have a long tail?

(from 234)

Answer 'Yes' if the tail made up at least one-sixth of its total length.

Yes 236   No 237

PINTAIL m
LONG-TAILED DUCK mw

R 66cm ewsi
W 53cm eSi

(from 235)

These two drakes are very dissimilar. The pintail is much the larger, though the tail of the long-tailed drake, which is a winter visitor, is considerably longer. The pintail is mainly grey-white, with a brown head, a white breast and a white stripe running up from the neck to behind the eye, while the long-tailed duck in winter is almost wholly black

and white. The latter is very much a sea bird, seldom seen inland, while the pintail is more a freshwater species but visits coastal marshes and estuaries in winter.

The two brownish females have shorter tails though they are more pointed than any others, and they are therefore considered separately (see 250 and 249 respectively).

Pintail
male

Long-tailed Duck
male

What colour was it?

(from 235)

Choose carefully which of these colour categories is appropriate.

All black 238
Mainly black and white 239

Head green/blue 240
Head or crown reddish brown 243
Mainly brown 246 None of these 251

---

238 **COMMON SCOTER** m   R 48cm EWSI

(from 237)

The common scoter is not very common. It is mainly a winter visitor but a few pairs stay the summer. Usually seen at sea some distance from the shore, often in flocks. The drake is all black with a yellow bill and can be confused only with the rarer velvet scoter (see the supplementary list), which is larger and has white wing-bars.

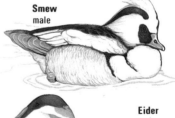

Common Scoter
male

The female scoter is brown and white (see 249).

---

239 **SMEW** m   W 41cm Es
GOLDENEYE m   W 46cm ewSi
(from 237)
  EIDER m   R 58cm ewSi

The smew and goldeneye are winter visitors. Both are most often seen on inland lakes and estuaries, more rarely on the open sea. The drake smew, when swimming, almost gives the appearance of being all white; in flight his black markings, especially his outer wings, show him to be pied. The female is grey with white cheeks and a dark brown cap (see 244).

The drake goldeneye has a green head, which in some lights may seem black. He is less white-looking than

the smew and much smaller than the eider with a quite differently shaped head. The white blob just in front of the eye is conspicuous. Goldeneye are more often seen on lakes but also occur on coastal waters. The female

Smew
male

Goldeneye
male

Eider
male

is grey with a reddish brown head (see 244).

The eider is much larger and is recognized by its unusual bill, which has a broader base than that of other ducks, running straight on into the forehead. The drake is conspicuously black and white with a faintly pink breast. Usually seen at sea. The female is mainly brown (see 250).

240 What size was it?

(from 237)

Of the six saltwater species with green heads (which in some cases may in certain lights seem blue), two are of average duck-size and four are above average. If you feel any doubt, glance at both entries.

Average for a duck 241
Above average for a duck 242

241 SCAUP m
GOLDENEYE m

(from 240)

W 48cm EWSI
W 46cm ewSi

Both are winter visitors. The drake scaup is reminiscent of the male tufted duck (see 201), but has a dark green instead of a dark brown head, and an all-grey back. Seen more often on estuaries than on open sea. The female is less conspicuous (see 249).

The goldeneye is more a lake bird, but also occurs on coastal waters. The drake's head is green, but in some lights may seem black, and there is a noticeable white blob just in front of the eye. The rest of his plumage is black and white. The

Scaup
male

Goldeneye
male

female is grey with a reddish brown head (see 244).

242 MALLARD m
SHELDUCK m-f
RED-BREASTED MERGANSER m
GOOSANDER m

(from 240)

R 58cm EWSI
R 61cm EWSI
R 58cm ewSI
R 66cm ewSi

The well-known mallard is the commonest freshwater duck but in winter is also seen on coastal waters and estuaries. The male is easily recognizable with his green head (which sometimes seems to be blue), white neckband, chestnut brown breast and bright blue speculum. The female is an inconspicuous brown with a blue speculum (see 247).

Shelduck are even more distinctive with their green heads, red beaks and legs, and gaudy chestnut/white/black plumage. The sexes are identical apart from the pronounced knob at the base of the drake's bill.

The red-breasted merganser and the goosander are less common than

Shelduck male

Mallard male

female

Goosander male

Red-breasted Merganser male

the other two. The latter is rarely seen in coastal waters. The two

drakes are rather similar but the merganser has a conspicuous double crest and a chestnut breast, while the goosander's neck and underparts are white tinged with pink, and his crest is barely noticeable. Both have long thin beaks with down-turned tips. For their respective females, see 245.

(from 237)

243	What size was it?

Of the six ducks with reddish-brown heads seen on coastal waters or estuaries, two are quite markedly above average size for a duck.

Average or below average for a duck 244

Above average for a duck 245

244	TEAL m	R 35cm EWSI
(from 243)	WIGEON m	R 46cm EWSI
	GOLDENEYE f	W 46cm ewSi
	SMEW f	W 41cm Es

The first three are mainly associated with lakes, but also visit estuaries or the sea, especially in winter. The smew, on the other hand, is very seldom seen inland, preferring sheltered coastal waters.

Only the teal is truly resident. The wigeon is primarily a winter visitor but a few birds stay the summer. The goldeneye and smew are exclusively winter visitors.

The drake teal is distinguished by his small size and by the bright green eye-stripe, edged with yellow, that runs back from his eye to his neck. For the brownish female, see 247. Teal are usually seen in flocks, and fly fast with rapid wing-beats in tight formation. The smallest British duck.

The drake wigeon is always most easily distinguished by the broad yellow stripe running back from his

Teal
male

Wigeon
male

Goldeneye
female

Smew
female

bill to his crown. Otherwise he has an all chestnut head and neck; the rest of his body is grey and white with a darker tail. He may be recognized in flight by the white stripe along the upper forewing. The female is mainly brown (see 247).

The head of the female goldeneye is chocolate brown. The rest of her body is light grey with white underparts. Goldeneye can always be distinguished in flight because their wings make a characteristic whistle. The male's head is dark green (see 241).

The dark brown head of the female smew does not extend below the level of the beak. The rest of the head is white, the rest of the body grey. For the very white-looking drake, see 201.

| 245 | RED-BREASTED MERGANSER f | R 58cm ewSl |
| | GOOSANDER f | R 66cm ewSi |

(from 243)

The red-breasted merganser may spend the summer either in coastal waters or inland, but in winter is found only by the sea. The goosander is primarily a bird of lakes and rivers but occasionally visits estuaries and coasts in winter.

These two females are not easy to distinguish. Both are crested: the merganser's is a double crest, the goosander's single. The goosander has a noticeably white throat, and therefore a greater contrast between throat and head. The green-headed drakes are more easily distinguished (see 242).

Red-breasted Merganser

female

Goosander
female

(from 237)

246   Did it have a blue or green speculum?

For an explanation of the word
'speculum', see 234.

Yes 247   No 248

Speculum

247

(from 246)

MALLARD f	R 58cm EWSI
TEAL f	R 35cm EWSI
WIGEON f	R 46cm EWSI

The mallard has a blue speculum, the teal and wigeon have green specula. Otherwise these three females are all-brown, and would be hard to tell apart if it were not for the size difference. The teal is the smallest British duck, the mallard one of the largest, while the wigeon comes midway between them. In each case

the drake is very distinctive – see 242 (mallard) and 244 (the others).

The wigeon is primarily a winter visitor, but a few birds stay all year.

Mallard
female

Wigeon
female

Teal
female

248   Did it have noticeable pale plumage on its head?

(from 246)

Three of the otherwise all-brown or brown/white females are distinguished by having patches of white or light grey feathers on their

heads, which in each case should have been noticed.

Yes 249   No 250

249

(from 248)

COMMON SCOTER f	R 48cm EWSI
SCAUP f	W 48cm EWSI
LONG-TAILED DUCK f	W 41cm eSi

All three are mainly birds of the open sea, though scoters, which are more often winter visitors, always nest inland if they stay for the summer.

The female scoter has the most obvious light head-patch and is otherwise dark brown. The all-black

drake is much more conspicuous (see 238). For the rarer velvet scoter, which has white wing-bars, see the supplementary list.

The female scaup has a small but noticeable pure white patch at the base of her bill. In flight her white

Common Scoter
female

Scaup
female

belly and broad white wing-bars are visible. As usual the drake is more easily distinguished (see 241).

The female long-tailed duck is the whitest of these three, with a mainly white head, neck, flanks and belly. She doesn't have the extremely long tail of the drake (see 236), which makes her smaller than all other ducks except the teal and garganey.

Long-tailed Duck
female

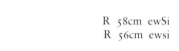

250	**EIDER** f	R 58cm ewSi
	PINTAIL f	R 56cm ewsi

(from 248)

These are the two least distinctive females and as usual are best recognized by reference to their drakes.

The eider is a true sea bird while the pintail is more often seen inland, especially in summer. When the pintail visits the coast in winter, it prefers estuaries and well-sheltered waters. The female eider is most easily distinguished by her heavy, broad-based bill, which closely

resembles the very conspicuous male's (see 239), and also by her sturdy build and heavily barred breast and flanks.

The fast-flying female pintail lacks the extremely long tail-feathers of the drake (see 236) but her tail is somewhat longer and more pointed than any of the others' and she is generally more slender and more delicate.

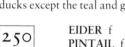

Eider
female

Pintail
female

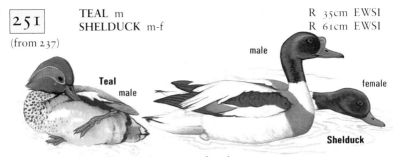

TEAL m   R 35cm EWSI
SHELDUCK m-f   R 61cm EWSI

The teal drake's head is mainly reddish-brown, but with such a conspicuous green eye-stripe, edged with yellow, that he is included here as well as at 244. Apart from these gaudy colours, teal are always distinguished by their very small size and rapid flight, usually in flocks. Much more often seen inland, but some birds visit coastal waters in winter. For the less distinctive female, see 247.

The shelduck also has a green head and is therefore included under 242; but in certain lights the green plumage may look black and the species is therefore repeated here. These large, handsome birds are very distinctive and should be instantly recognized. The sexes are alike apart from the large knob at the base of the drake's bill.

Was it a gull or tern?

Gulls and terns are recognizable as such because they are mainly white and pearl grey. Though some species have black wing-tips and others have backs and upper wings that are wholly black or dark grey, they all have a generally white appearance.

Both families have long pointed wings, but the terns' are even longer and narrower than the gulls'. Terns are also distinguished by their forked tails (not square), their black crowns and their more delicate flight.

Furthermore, gulls are surface feeders, while terns sometimes dive into the water to seek small fish under the surface.

Gull 253   Tern 260
Neither of these 261

What colour were its back and upper wings?

Carefully choose which colour category is appropriate.

Black or very dark grey 254
Mainly grey or white 255
Brown/white 259

(from 208 and 253)

Lesser Black-backed Gull

Great Black-backed Gull

These two large gulls are instantly told from all others by their black upperparts (great black-backed) or very dark grey upperparts (lesser black-backed). In certain lights this difference in colour cannot be made out and both species look wholly black and white. They can then be distinguished by the noticeably greater size of the great black-backed gull (which is variable – from 64–79cm) and by its pink legs; the lesser black-backed gull's are yellow. Neither species is usually gregarious, except at nesting sites. Like other gulls, they are both scavengers, often found near rubbish dumps.

---

255 Did it have black feathers in its wing-tips?

(from 253)

Answer 'Yes' if the wing-tips were solid black, black with white spots, or no more than edged with black.   Yes 256 No 258

---

256 Did it have a yellow head and neck?

(from 255)

This question needs no elaboration.   Yes 275 No 257

257	BLACK-HEADED GULL mfs-mfw	R 37cm EWSI
	COMMON GULL mf	R 41cm EWSI
(from 208	KITTIWAKE mf	R 41cm eWSI
and 256)	HERRING GULL mf	R 61cm EWSI

The first two are misleadingly named because the black-headed gull has in fact a chocolate brown head, which becomes white in winter apart from a small brown spot behind the eye, and the common gull is not very common.

Apart from its brown head in summer, the black-headed gull can be distinguished in all seasons by its smaller size, its more delicate flight and its bright red beak and legs. Its outer wings are edged with black. The legs of the common gull are greenish yellow and it has white-spotted black wing-tips.

The kittiwake is something like the common gull but is distinguished from it by its solid black wing-tips, more delicate tern-like flight and, if standing, by its black legs and feet. It usually spends the winter far out at sea and, in summer, breeds in colonies, usually on cliffs, where its loud cries of '*kitt-ee-wake*' immediately draw attention.

The very common herring gull is quite similar to both, but is sturdier and noticeably larger, varying from 56–66cm. Furthermore its legs are usually pinkish and it has a prominent red spot on its heavy yellow beak.

Black-headed Gull in winter

Common Gull

Black-headed Gull

summer

Kittiwake

Herring Gull

(from 255)

| 258 | FULMAR mf | R 47cm ewsi |

Fulmars are tubenoses not gulls, but they are certainly gull-like (apart from their hooked bills and rather stiff-winged flight) and are therefore dealt with here. They spend all their lives at sea, frequently out of sight of land, except when nesting. They almost always nest on cliffs in colonies. They are the only sea birds to have wholly grey upper wings without black tips; their heads, necks

Fulmar

and underparts are predominantly white.

| 259 | Immature Gulls |

(from 253)

Almost all immature gulls are mainly brown and white. This plumage varies according to age. They are very hard to distinguish and are considered beyond the scope of this book.

The only other possibility is that it wasn't a gull but a skua (see 273).

260

(from 297
and 252)

COMMON TERN mf
ARCTIC TERN mf
SANDWICH TERN mf

S 35cm EwSI
S 35cm ewSi
S 41cm EwSI

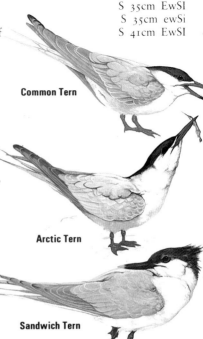

Common Tern

Arctic Tern

Sandwich Tern

The common tern and arctic tern are almost impossible to tell apart, except in the hand. The most important distinction is that the arctic tern has an all-red bill, while the common tern's is red with a black tip, but this very small difference can seldom be made out.

The common tern is slightly smaller, has slightly longer legs and a shorter tail; but again these differences are almost negligible. However, the arctic tern is so much scarcer that you will have to assume it was a common tern unless you can establish definitely that it wasn't.

The upperparts of the sandwich tern, like the others', are grey, but the bill is black with a yellow tip, and a slight crest may be noticeable. Its legs and feet (black, not red) are also very distinctive.

261

Did it have webbed feet?

(from 252)

If it was swimming, you can be sure that it had webbed feet; and all the remaining web-footed species are invariably seen swimming in the sea or flying over it, almost always some distance from the shore, unless they are on rocks or cliffs by the very edge of the sea.

Yes 262   No 276

262

Was it a member of the diver family?

(from 261)

Members of the diver family spend almost all their lives either swimming or diving, coming ashore only to nest. They have a generally streamlined appearance, their heads merging easily into their necks, their necks into their bodies, and they have quite long pointed bills. If in

Divers

doubt, turn first to 263 before proceeding to 264.

Yes 263   No 264

GREAT NORTHERN DIVER mfw   W 76cm ewSi
BLACK-THROATED DIVER mfs-mfw   R 63cm ewS
RED-THROATED DIVER mfs-mfw   R 56cm ewSi

The great northern diver is a winter visitor and the black-throated diver normally nests beside fresh water, so the red-throated diver is usually the only member of the family to be seen on or near the sea in its more distinctive summer uniform, with its grey neck and chestnut neck-patch.

Apart from the difference in their sizes, which are variable, these three species are hard to distinguish in winter. All are predominantly brown with white underparts, but the red-throated diver – more delicate and usually smaller than the others – is lighter in colour and its back is flecked with white. It has a slightly up-turned bill. The black-throated diver comes midway in size and is more heavily built. The great northern diver has a straight heavy bill and is much larger.

Great Northern Diver
winter

summer

winter

Black-throated Diver

Red-throated Diver

winter

summer

What colour was it?

Carefully choose the correct colour category. Choose 'mainly black' even if there were extensive areas of white.

Head reddish-brown or green [265]

Mainly black (or very dark brown) [266]
Brown and white only [273]
Light grey and white, some black [274]
White, yellow head [275]

RED-BREASTED MERGANSER m-f   R 58cm ewSI
GOOSANDER m-f   R 66cm ewSi

Goosander   female

female

male

male

Red-breasted Merganser

Both these species are in fact larger-than-usual members of the duck family but are repeated here in case they were not recognized as such. In both cases the male has a greenish head and the female's is reddish-brown, and both species have long, thin bills with down-turned tips. The goosander is much more often seen on inland waters, but occasionally visits coastal waters and estuaries in winter, where the merganser may more commonly be seen all year.

The goosander drake has a hardly perceptible crest; the duck has a single crest. The male and female mergansers both have double crests, and the drake is further distinguished by his conspicuous reddish-brown breast. By contrast the male goosander has a white breast and underparts, slightly tinged with pink.

Both drakes have a noticeably black-and-white appearance, especially in flight. The ducks are a less conspicuous grey. The female goosander has a sharp division between her brown head and her white neck and throat; the transition is much more gradual in the merganser. Both species are very good divers.

266

(from 264)

Did it have quite extensive white plumage?

Answer 'Yes' unless any white plumage was confined to the head only.   Yes 267   No 272

267

(from 266)

Was it smaller than a blackbird?

Two species of these black-and-white sea birds are very noticeably smaller than the others, which are all at least half as big again.   Yes 268   No 269

STORM PETREL mf   S 15cm ewsi
LEACH'S PETREL mf   S 20cm ewsi

Storm Petrel

These two species belong mainly to the open ocean, far out of sight of land; but sometimes they visit coastal waters in summer, and come ashore to nest at a few locations in the British Isles. They may be seen fluttering daintily just above the waves, usually in small flocks. Both are mainly dark brown, which often gives the appearance of being black.

The storm petrel is much commoner and is distinguished by its smaller size. It is little bigger than a house martin (see 182), which it rather resembles, with its long pointed wings and conspicuous white rump. It also has rather more white in its upper wings, and a square tail. Leach's petrel also has a white rump,

Leach's Petrel

but its tail is forked. A very infrequent visitor.

Did it have a huge, multi-coloured bill?

This question needs no elaboration.   Yes 270 No 271

PUFFIN mfs-mfw   R 30cm eWSI

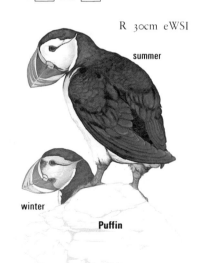

summer

winter

Puffin

The remarkable black and white puffin is immediately recognized by its outrageously large bill, striped yellow, black and red. Ashore, it has an upright stance, almost like a penguin. It has a large head and bright red legs. Usually seen in flocks.

Puffins come ashore to nest in burrows at selected coastal locations, sometimes in huge colonies. In winter their white cheeks are darker; and their bills, though still enormous, are a little bit smaller and less brilliantly coloured.

RAZORBILL mfs-mfw	R 41cm eWSI
GUILLEMOT mfs-mfw	R 42cm eWSI
BLACK GUILLEMOT mfs	R 34cm ewSI
MANX SHEARWATER mf	S 35cm ewsI

The first three, which are auks, are strong, heavy birds, seen on cliffs and rocks as often as swimming or flying.

The razorbill and guillemot may at first sight seem very similar, with all-black upperparts and all-white underparts, but they are immediately distinguished by their bills. The razorbill's is very large and heavy, flattened vertically in a rather curious way, black flecked with white, while the guillemot's is slender and pointed. Both species are whiter in winter. The much scarcer little auk

looks like a small guillemot (see the supplementary list).

When in its breeding plumage, the black guillemot is all black except for a conspicuous white patch on the upper wing. In winter it is mainly grey and white (see 274).

The manx shearwater, an uncommon summer visitor, is wholly different. Delicate and gull-like in appearance, with long pointed wings, it is usually seen flying low above the waves. It is all black above and mainly white below.

Razorbill
summer
winter

Guillemot
summer
winter

Black Guillemot
summer

Manx Shearwater

CORMORANT mf
SHAG mf

R 90cm EWSI
R 76cm eWSI

Both species normally look black, and are the only sea birds except scoters to do so, though the cormorant has inconspicuous white patches on its cheeks and thighs. Both are in fact dark brown, with a slight greenish tinge. They have long yellow bills, turned down at the ends.

The two species are told apart by the great difference in size; the shag, which is less common, also has a smaller head and flies with faster wing-beats. Both are strong divers. In flight, with their long necks outstretched, they resemble large black ducks.

Shag

Cormorant

ARCTIC SKUA mf
GREAT SKUA mf

S 46cm ewSi
S 58cm ewsi

Skuas look like immature gulls, with their brown and white plumage and long pointed wings, but they have characteristic wedge-shaped tails and a rather less delicate flight, though when chasing other sea birds (as is their habit) they show much agility and speed. They spend winter far out at sea, but may be seen in coastal waters in summer or as passage migrants in spring and autumn.

The arctic skua is the commoner of the two and is a confusing species because its neck and underparts may vary in colour from white to very dark brown. The two longish feathers projecting from its tail may not be noticed. The great skua is larger, more heavily built, with broader wings and prominent white wing patches. Both species – but especially the arctic – have breeding sites scattered round our coast, mainly in Scotland.

Great Skua

dark form

light form

Arctic Skua

BLACK GUILLEMOT mfw

R 34cm ewSI

(from 264)

Black Guillemot
winter

The black guillemot in summer is quite distinctive (see 271) with its almost all-black plumage. But in winter this disappears, apart from some black areas in its wings and tail. It retains its white wing patches but its upperparts become predominantly grey and its underparts, including its throat and breast, pure white. Flies with rapid wing-beats and tends to stay quite close inshore.

275 **GANNET** mf

R 90cm EWSI

(from 256 and 264)

Gannets are at once recognized by their yellow heads, their great size, their distinctive long, pointed bills, their white wings with solid black tips, and by the way they fish – diving into the sea from a considerable height, head first and wings folded.

Gannet

276 Was it a wader?

(from 261)

The sixteen species of wader considered under this heading have long legs and rather long bills. They are seen wading in shallow water, walking or standing near water or marshy ground, or flying low over it. They usually have a rapid, often zigzag flight.

Note that the heron sometimes wades, and is long-legged and long-

Waders

billed, but is not classed among the waders. It is very large (90cm), and mainly grey with a long neck (see 288).

Yes 277 No 286

277 Did it have any black plumage?

(from 276)

Of the species considered, three are conspicuously pied black and white, while four others have noticeable black areas on the head or breast.

For all these, turn to 278; otherwise to 281.

Yes 278 No 281

Was it smaller than a blackbird?

(from 277)

Decide whether it was smaller than
the very well-known blackbird
(25cm) or quite definitely bigger.　　Yes 279 No 280

279	DUNLIN mfs	R 18cm EWSI
	LITTLE RINGED PLOVER mf	S 15cm E
(from 278)	RINGED PLOVER mf	R 19cm EWSI
	TURNSTONE mfs-mfw	R 23cm ewsi

The first three are much smaller than
other waders – hardly bigger than
chaffinches.

The dunlin in summer has a
distinguishing black belly. Its bill
turns slightly downward. Dunlin
almost always breed inland; when
occurring on the coast, they are
usually confined to mud-flats. For the
less conspicuous winter plumage, see
282.

The two plovers are instantly
recognized by the black-and-white
markings on their heads and breasts.
The size difference is appreciable and
the ringed plover has a pale wing-bar
which is quite noticeable in flight,
and its bill is red with a black tip.
Moreover the little ringed plover, a
summer visitor, nests inland, and is
seen only occasionally at the coast,
almost always on mud-flats. The
ringed plover is quite common all
year, usually on the seashore, but in
winter also occurs on estuaries.

The turnstone is primarily a
winter visitor, but a few birds are
present all year. In both its plumages,
it has quite noticeable black and
white areas, and it is larger than both
the plovers – almost blackbird-size. It
almost always occurs on stony
beaches, where (as its name implies)
it may be seen turning the stones in
search of food. Usually seen in small
flocks, often with other waders.

Dunlin
summer

Little
Ringed
Plover

Ringed
Plover

winter

Turnstone

summer

280	OYSTERCATCHER mf	R 43cm EWSI
	LAPWING mf	R 30cm EWSI
(from 278)	AVOCET mf	R 43cm ewi

Near the sea, the oystercatcher is the
commonest of these three

conspicuous species, and is easily
recognized by its striking pied

plumage, long bright red bill and pink legs. It is about the size of a rook. In summer it is usually seen on stony beaches, or in fields or marshland near the sea; in winter on estuaries and mud-flats.

The much smaller lapwing, also known as the peewit or green plover, is common enough inland; it occurs far less often on mud-flats or beaches, usually in winter and often in large flocks. It is crested and has distinctive pied plumage, which in

some lights has a distinctly greenish sheen.

If you are lucky enough to have sighted an avocet, you are hardly likely to mistake it. It's the most boldly pied of all, mainly pure white with a black crown and black-barred wings, and particularly distinguished by its long upturned bill and its very long legs. The avocet usually nests in marshland by the sea. Outside the breeding season, it may be seen on mud-flats and estuaries.

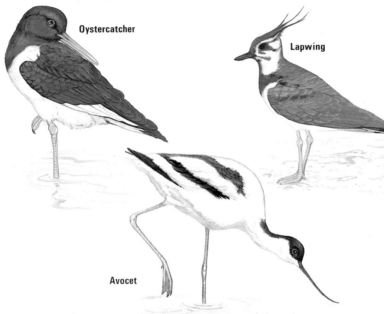

Oystercatcher

Lapwing

Avocet

281 Was it generally greyish-brown?

(from 277)

The ten remaining waders are all predominantly brown or brown and white. It is no good pretending that they are easy to distinguish, but in four of them the brown plumage is quite definitely greyish. Extremely

careful observation is necessary and you may have to search back and forth between 282, 284 and 285 before arriving at a conclusion.

Yes 282 No 283

DUNLIN mfw
SANDERLING mfw
KNOT mfw
GREY PLOVER mfw

R 18cm EWSI
W 20cm EWSI
W 25cm ewsi
W 28cm Ewsi

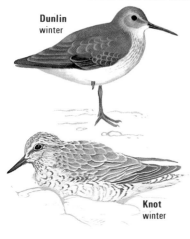

Dunlin
winter

Knot
winter

Sanderling
winter

Grey Plover
winter

The dunlin in winter is less distinctive than in the breeding season (see 279). So are the three others, but they are winter visitors, too seldom seen here in their summer finery to be included in it.

In their winter plumage, all four species are far from conspicuous and hard to distinguish. The dunlin is the commonest and smallest – little bigger than a chaffinch – while its colour is more brownish than the others. It is usually seen in flocks, flying rapidly and erratically in tight formation, and is most at home on mud-flats and coastal marshes.

The sanderling is slightly larger and, as its name implies, is virtually always seen on sandy beaches, where it has a way of racing in and out with each succeeding breaker. It is distinguished by its very white appearance, the whitest of all the shore-birds, with grey-white crown and upperparts.

The knot and grey plover are blackbird-sized. Like the sanderling, they are both seen on sandy beaches but also occur on muddy shores and estuaries. The plover has a shorter, thicker bill and is distinguished by its noticeable white rump, slightly barred white tail and very pale underparts. Both species have light eye-stripes.

| 283 |

Was it about the size of a blackbird?

Answer 'Yes' if it was the size of a blackbird (25cm) or not much bigger. Answer 'No' if it was unmistakably much larger.

Yes 284   No 285

GOLDEN PLOVER mfw   R 28cm EWSI
REDSHANK mf .   R 28cm EwSi
GREENSHANK mf   R 30cm ewSi
GREEN SANDPIPER mf   W 23cm EWsi

Golden Plover winter

Green Sandpiper

Redshank

Greenshank

It is only in winter that these four species are likely to be seen on estuaries or the coast.

The golden plover in its winter plumage is plain speckled brown with white underparts, easily told from the others by its much shorter bill. For its more distinctive summer plumage, see 221.

The three others all have white rumps. The redshank has long red legs, a black-tipped red bill, and a white wing-bar on the trailing edge of its upper wings, noticeable in flight. The greenshank is lighter-coloured with no wing-bar. Its long legs are brownish with only a hint of green.

In flight both these species utter a characteristic three-note whistle – '*peep . . . peep . . . peep*'.

The green sandpiper, a winter visitor or passage migrant, is the least common of these, and noticeably the smallest. Its upperparts are much darker than the others, as are the undersides of its wings. It has a barred tail and a quite noticeable pale eye-stripe.

Misleadingly named, because it has no green plumage.

CURLEW mf   R 56cm EWSI
WHIMBREL mf   R 41cm ewsi

Curlew

Whimbrel

These two species are very much alike in colour and outline, but the curlew is much bigger.

Both have long legs and very long, down-turned bills. The curlew has a rather inconspicuous white rump, while the whimbrel, which flies with faster wing-beats, has distinctive striped head-markings. Both species like mud-flats.

Whimbrels are usually seen as passage migrants in spring and autumn; a few stay all year.

286   What colour was it?

(from 276)

The six remaining species all belong quite clearly to one or other of the colour categories below, from which you should have no difficulty in choosing.

All black, red bill and legs 287
Mainly grey 288
Blue-grey, white rump 289
Brown and white 290

287   CHOUGH mf   R 39cm ewsi

(from 286)

The chough is found exclusively on cliffs along the coast. It is an all-black bird and belongs to the same family as the rook and crow, with which it might be confused, if it were not for its bright red legs, its long, down-curved, bright red bill and its smaller size.

Chough

288   GREY HERON mf   R 90cm EWSI
(from 286)   **PEREGRINE** m   R 38cm ewsi
         PEREGRINE f   R 48cm ewsi

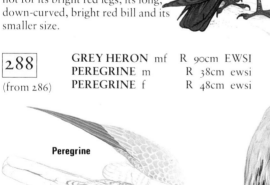

Peregrine

Grey Heron

The heron is at once distinguished from all other species by its very great size, long legs and very long neck, which is retracted in flight. Its black crest and wing feathers are not at all conspicuous and it gives the impression of being all grey and white. When fishing, it stands stock still, sometimes on one leg, often in shallow water. Much more a freshwater species but sometimes occurs on seashore or on estuaries.

The peregrine is very different. It is a falcon with long pointed wings and a fast, dashing flight, sometimes aerobatic, sometimes plunging earthwards, in a typical 'anchor'-shape, after prey. Note that the sexes are almost identical except for the considerable difference in size. The upperparts are grey except for the black wing-tips, while the underparts are white, barred with brown. Likes cliffs and rocky coasts.

| 289 | ROCK DOVE mf | R 33cm eSI |

(from 286)

This is the one member of the dove family that is almost wholly confined to sea cliffs. It has the same general blue-grey colour as the stock dove and woodpigeon, but is clearly told from them (apart from its habitat) by its conspicuous white rump.

Rock Dove

| 290 | ROCK PIPIT mf
SNOW BUNTING m-f | R 16.5cm EWSI
W 16.5cm ewSi |

(from 286)

These two small birds cannot be confused. The rock pipit, which is very much the commoner, is an inconspicuous speckled brown, and resembles other members of its undistinguished family (see 12). But if it was on the shore, you can be almost certain that it was a rock pipit.

The snow bunting, a winter visitor, sometimes occurs inland, but is usually seen on the coast. A fairly rare visitor, its winter plumage is mainly white – this is specially noticeable in flight – with an intermingling of brown, which is rather darker in the male than in the female. Usually seen in flocks.

Rock Pipit

female

male
(winter)

Snow Bunting

male
(summer)

Supplementary List

If you have failed to find your bird in the main body of the book, look at this list of the 38 next most common species. Only the barest details to aid identification are given.

LAND BIRDS

Under 15cm

FIRECREST m-f R 9cm e
Tiny. No bigger than goldcrest (see 60), from which distinguished by black/white eyestripes.

Firecrest male · female

Dartford Warbler

Cirl Bunting male · female

DARTFORD WARBLER m-f
R 12.5cm e
Reddish breast, grey upperparts and head. Cocked-up tail. Likes bushes, especially gorse. Very shy.

16-25cm

Residents
CIRL BUNTING m-f R 16cm e
Heavy beak. Male has striking head pattern, female plainer. Hedgerows and bushes.

HAWFINCH m-f R 18cm ews
Extremely heavy beak, bright colouring. Likes deciduous woodland and gardens. Secretive.

Hawfinch

Wryneck

male

female

Red-backed Shrike

Dotterel summer

Waxwing

Great Grey Shrike

Hobby

Summer visitors
WRYNECK mf S 16cm es
Brown with grey back and head,
barred tail. Very shrill call.
Deciduous woodland and gardens.
Nests in hole.

RED-BACKED
SHRIKE mf S 17cm es
Very distinctive colouring. Often
chooses a prominent perch. Rough
scrubby country.

DOTTEREL mfs S 23cm es
A wader but prefers dry ground in
summer. Distinctive colouring with
pronounced white eye-stripes.

Winter visitors
WAXWING mf W 18cm esi
Very bright colouring with
conspicuous crest. Often seen feeding
on berries.

GREAT GREY
SHRIKE mf W 24cm es
Conspicuous grey/black/white
plumage. Sometimes hovers. Open
country and woodland.

<u>26-46cm</u>
HOBBY m-f S 30cm (m)-36cm
(f) e
A falcon, with long narrow wings
and short tail. Boldly streaked breast
and reddish 'trousers'.

RED-LEGGED PARTRIDGE mf R 33cm ew
Plump and rounded with black/white head pattern and barred flanks. Fields and open country, usually in coveys.

STONE CURLEW mf S 40cm e
Almost crow-size. Long yellow legs, otherwise rather undistinguished. Flies with legs dangling. Open country.

Over 46cm
Owl

SNOWY OWL m-f R 53cm (m) 66cm (f) s
Unmistakable very large owl with mainly pure white plumage.

Red-legged Partridge

Stone Curlew

Snowy Owl

Osprey

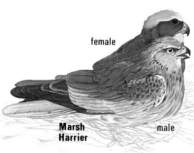

female

Marsh Harrier

male

Birds of prey

MARSH HARRIER m-f R 48-56cm e
Mainly a summer visitor. Male noticeably brown/grey with black wing-tips, female all brown/white. Prefers wet country but sometimes visits farmland.

OSPREY m-f S 51-58cm es
Pure white underparts and 'trousers'. Prefers wooded country with lakes or rivers. Hovers before diving for prey.

RED KITE m-f R 61-63cm ew
Confined almost exclusively to
Welsh mountains. Large with forked
tail.

GOLDEN EAGLE m-f R 76-
89cm es
The largest bird of prey. Seldom
occurs outside Scottish Highlands.
Often soars and glides. All brown,
powerful claws and bill.

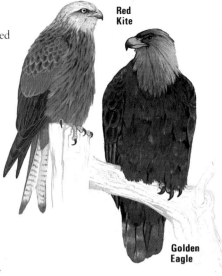

Red
Kite

Golden
Eagle

WATER BIRDS

Under 15cm
LITTLE STINT mfs-mfw
*P 13cm ewsi
Very small wader. Rather short,
straight bill. Estuaries, also inland.

16-25cm
Residents
BEARDED TIT m-f R 16cm e
Long tail. Male has conspicuous
head pattern. Prefers extensive reed
beds. Often in flocks outside
breeding season.

Summer visitors
RED-NECKED PHALAROPE ms-
fs S 18cm esi
Coasts, islands, marshes and lake
shores. Longish bill, conspicuous
scarlet neck.

winter

Little
Stint

summer

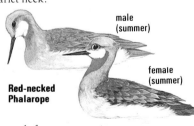

male
(summer)

female
(summer)

**Red-necked
Phalarope**

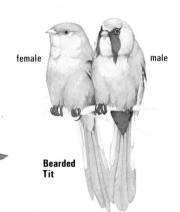

female

male

**Bearded
Tit**

*P stands for *passage migrant* –
usually seen only *on passage* (i.e.
when migrating) in spring or
autumn.

WOOD SANDPIPER mf S 20cm ewsi
Prefers fresh water: marshes, lake shores, reservoirs. Inconspicuous wader, with yellow legs and white rump.

LITTLE TERN mf S 24cm ewsi
Sea bird. Like other terns (see 260) but much smaller. Yellow bill, tipped with black.

BLACK TERN mfs P 24cm esi
Sea bird. Like other terns (see 260) but extensive black/grey plumage makes it unmistakable. Same size as little tern.

Wood Sandpiper

Little Tern

Black Tern

Winter visitors
LITTLE AUK mfw W 20cm es
Sea bird. Like a very small razorbill (see 271), but with short bill.

Passage migrants*
CURLEW SANDPIPER mfs-mfw P 19cm ewsi
Marshes and mud-flats. Wader with down-curved bill. May be seen in either summer plumage (brown) or winter plumage (grey). Has a white rump.

*Passage migrants (indicated by abbreviation P) are usually seen only *on passage* (i.e. when migrating) in spring and autumn.

winter   summer

Little Auk

Curlew Sandpiper

winter

summer

PURPLE SANDPIPER mfs-
mfw P 21cm ewsi
Short yellow legs. Dark plumage,
sometimes with purplish sheen.
Rocky shores, piers and breakwaters.

26-46cm
Grebes
Grebes are seen on inland waters all
year, and on estuaries and coasts in
winter.

BLACK-NECKED GREBE mfs-
mfw R 30cm ewsi
Summer: generally black in
appearance with yellow ear-tufts.
Winter: dusky with white
underparts. Up-turned bill.

SLAVONIAN GREBE mfs-
mfw R 33cm ewsi
Like black-necked grebe, but with
chestnut ear tufts, neck and flanks in
summer, generally paler in winter.
Down-turned bill.

**RED-NECKED
GREBE** mfw W 43cm es
Winter: like the two above but
larger. Almost black crown, white
cheeks, yellow bill. Seldom seen
inland. No red neck in winter.

summer
winter

**Purple
Sandpiper**

Black-necked Grebe

summer

winter

winter

Slavonian Grebe

summer

winter

summer

Red-necked Grebe

Waders

SPOTTED REDSHANK mfs-
mfw W 30cm ewsi
Bright red legs. Very dark plumage in
summer, sometimes seen here when
on passage, turning in winter to pale
grey with white eye-stripes and
underparts.

summer

winter

Spotted Redshank

BLACK-TAILED GODWIT mfs-
mfw R 40cm ewsi
Looks like bar-tailed godwit, but
almost straight bill and black tail.
Seen all year on mud-flats and coasts
in summer also on marshy ground
inland.

summer

Bar-tailed Godwit

winter

winter

summer

Black-tailed Godwit

BAR-TAILED GODWIT mfs-
mfw W 38cm ewsi
Very scarce in summer. Slightly up-
turned bill. In winter very pale with
barred tail. Estuaries and seashores.

Gulls and terns

LITTLE GULL mfw W 28cm ews
Seldom seen inland. Very small, tern-
like gull. Smokey grey underwings.
Head and neck, jet black in summer
are grey/white in winter.

Little Gull

ROSEATE TERN mf S 38cm ewsi
Sea bird. Like other terns (see 260)
but breast has pinkish tinge. Strong
black bill; extra long tail.

Roseate Tern

Fresh water

MARSH HARRIER m-f R 48cm
(m) 56cm (f) e
Mainly a summer visitor. Male
noticeably brown/grey with black
wing-tips, female all brown/white.
Prefers wet country but sometimes
visits farmland.

OSPREY m-f S 50cm (m) 58cm
(f) es
Pure white underparts and 'trousers'.
Prefers wooded country with lakes or
rivers. Hovers before diving for prey.

BEAN GOOSE mf W 71-89cm es
Fields near inland water. Very plain
goose, mostly brown, with black-
tipped yellow bill and yellow legs.
Variable size.

BITTERN mf R 76cm ew
Very secretive. Reed beds and
undergrowth near fresh water.
Strong yellow bill. Strange booming
'song' may be heard at great
distances.

Salt water

VELVET SCOTER m-f
W 56cm es
Sea bird. Very similar to common
scoter (see 238/249) but larger; and
both sexes have white wing-bar and
white eye-patch.

GLAUCOUS GULL mf W
63-81cm esi
Sea bird. Very large gull, grey/white
with no dark plumage. Pink legs and
yellow bill. Variable size.

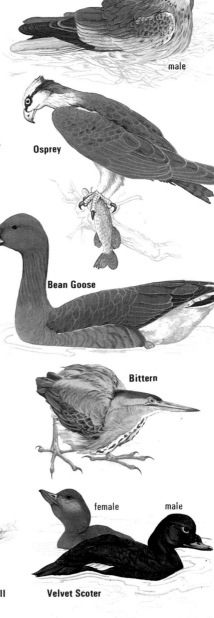

Marsh
Harrier female

male

Osprey

Bean Goose

Bittern

female   male

Velvet Scoter

Glaucous Gull

Key

If you feel you no longer need the help of the Questions, you may find it more convenient to use the abbreviated key below, which should lead you more quickly to your Answer.

LAND BIRDS

CHAFFINCH-SIZE OR SMALLER

Brown or brown/white	Open country	Thin-billed 6
		Thick-billed 13
	Not open country	White wing-marks 14
		No white wing-marks 17

Ignore brown/white, choose which other colour predominates

Black	Mainly black/white	Swallow-like 89
		Not swallow-like 26
	Not mainly black/white	29
Grey	Long tail	97
	No long tail	39
Red	Long tail	27
	No long tail	Red breast 51
		No red breast 58
Yellow/green .	Extremely small	60
	Not extremely small	Tit family 62
		Not tit family 63
Blue	62	

BIGGER THAN CHAFFINCH, NOT BIGGER THAN BLACKBIRD

Brown or brown/white .	Owl	74
	Snipe	76
	Neither of above	Nearer to chaffinch 78
		Nearer to blackbird 86

Ignore brown/white, choose which other colour predominates

Black	Swallow-like	89
	Not swallow-like	Wholly black 91
		Not wholly black 92
Grey	Long tail	97
	No long tail	98
Red	101	
Yellow	Long tail	191
	No long tail	107
Green	108	

BIGGER THAN BLACKBIRD, NOT BIGGER THAN ROOK

Jay	111	
Dove	Blue/grey, purple	114
	Brownish	115
Bird of prey ..	Brown/white	118
	Brown/blue-grey	121
	Mainly grey	122

WATER BIRDS

On or near Fresh Water
BLACKBIRD-SIZE OR SMALLER

BIGGER THAN A BLACKBIRD

On or near Salt Water

Index and Checklist

Use the boxes to mark with an 'x' each new species as you see it. There are spare boxes at the end for you to insert rare species that are not included.

SL indicates that the species is in the Supplementary List at the end of the book.

☐ ....
☐ ....
☐ ....
☐ ....
☐ ....
☐ ....
☐ ....
☐ ....
☐ ....
☐ ....
☐ ....
☐ ....
☐ ....
☐ ....
☐ ....
☐ ....

Notes

t
"p
to
reg

Notes

Notes